1970

This book may be kept

TEN DAYS

THE CASE OF EZRA POUND

THE CASE OF
EZRA POUND

___

by *Charles Norman*

To the reader:

"This book makes an important contribution to the literature about Ezra Pound. It brings into perspective the documentary material concerning his treason case as seen by Mr. Norman, his biographer. Mr. Norman has included in this book sympathetic and detailed commentary about Pound the man and Pound the poet."

—JULIEN CORNELL (attorney for Pound during the treason case and author of a documentary book about Pound's case entitled *The Trial of Ezra Pound*, John Day Company).

Funk and Wagnalls, New York

TO SAMUEL P. SHAW, JR.

Contents

	Foreword	ix
one	The Man Who Hated England	3
two	The Poet	14
three	The Antithetical Self	26
four	The Monetary Reformer	36
five	The Propagandist	47
six	United States *vs.* Ezra Pound	62
seven	Points of View	83
eight	For the Defense	92
nine	Morning Session: Dr. Wendell Muncie	106
ten	Morning Session: Dr. Marion R. King	129
eleven	Morning and Afternoon: Dr. Winfred Overholser	146
twelve	Afternoon Session: Dr. Joseph L. Gilbert	163
thirteen	Constitutional Questions	181
fourteen	Dismissal of Indictment	190
	Postscript	200
	Index	205

Foreword

On November 18, 1945, Ezra Pound was flown from Italy and confined in the District of Columbia jail to await trial for broadcasting enemy propaganda "contrary to his duty of allegiance to the United States." He was sixty years old.

Four psychiatrists—three for the government, the other acting in behalf of the defendant—found unanimously that he was "mentally unfit to advise properly with counsel or to participate intelligently and reasonably in his own defense." How commendable are the safeguards written into Anglo-Saxon and American law; yet there were those who believed the government did not wish to try Pound for treason and had found a way out.

The opposite was true. The Department of Justice asked for a statutory inquisition on the sanity issue, and this was held before Chief Judge Bolitha J. Laws of the United States District Court, District of Columbia, and a jury. The witnesses were the same four psychiatrists, whose original conclusions could not be shaken in cross-examination. A glance at their testimony will show how hard the government tried—always with restraint and fairness— to find a basis for putting Pound on trial. He was remanded instead to St. Elizabeths Hospital, a government institution, where, as Criminal No. 76028, he remained until April 18, 1958, when the indictment was dismissed and he was released in the custody of his wife, with whom he returned to Italy.

The case of Ezra Pound will always be interesting, not only because the central figure was a noted poet, but also because there were issues, unnoticed by most, that in the end loomed as large as the crime for which he was indicted. I leave the documents to speak for themselves, with occasional comments; others might have been wiser had they done the same, for every attempt to show him as a victim, through suppression of facts, incenses the public anew against Pound.

There was no victimization. What is open to question is the incarceration, seemingly for life, of an accused man who had not been tried. This aspect of the story is fully covered here as is the government's case, which appears to have been formidable. Mrs. Pound, it may be thought, was unfortunate in stating in writing that "the treason was in the White House, not in Rapallo," on which Pound commented to the present writer: "She is quoting E. P." His partisans have repeated it, with embellishments of their own, but with as little evidence.

I thank the Bureau of Intelligence and Research, Department of State, for help in getting important material declassified for this book; The Adjutant General's Office, Department of the Army; the World War II Records Division of the National Archives and Records Service; the Library of Congress; the American Civil Liberties Union; and RAI Corporation, the Italian Radio TV System.

Grateful acknowledgments are due to Mr. Julien Cornell and Mr. Thurman Arnold, Pound's lawyers in 1945 and 1958, respectively. In his Affidavit in Support of Application for Bail, Mr. Cornell had the following note: "In order to furnish the Court with further information about the defendant, if desired, I have appended as Exhibit A, a copy of the only material concerning him which has been published currently, namely, an article which appeared in the newspaper *PM* (New York) for November 25, 1945."

That article, "The Case For and Against Ezra Pound," of which I was the author, was an account of Pound's life and work up to that time. In quoting from the affidavit, I have avoided repetition of material incorporated in my narrative. Included in the article were contributions by other writers whose views I had invited; these will be found in Chapter seven.

C. N.

THE CASE OF EZRA POUND

one

The Man Who Hated England

---------- **1** ----------

"The case is also of some human interest, for it illustrates the dangers of anti-Semitism. Any negative belief, enthusiastically held, which is based on prejudice and not on evidence, is apt to be dangerous, and if in addition it is founded on hatred, it may well prove to have disastrous consequences on the judgment and outlook of those who hold it."
SOLICITOR–GENERAL, THE EARL JOWITT, "The Case of Tyler Kent," in *Some Were Spies*, London, 1954

He was five feet, ten and a half inches tall. He wore a hat with a wide brim and a double-breasted overcoat with broad lapels scissoring downward to three rows of buttons, the top two rows of

3

which were left unbuttoned. One side of his shirt collar was turned up, Regency style, but the other side—the left—was turned down and its point allowed, or made, to flap over the left overcoat lapel. In plain view a tie big as a sash, and casually looped, descended to the lower depths of a double-breasted jacket.

The man thus attired entered a Renaissance-style building on the Via Asiago and took off his hat, holding it by the brim against his side. His thick, curly hair, once a reddish gold, was cropped at the sides and made a mound which appeared to rise in tiers. Mustache and a scant beard merely gave an unkempt look to the round, flabby face, but there were deep grooves beside the straight nose and furrows in the wide brow. The green eyes were sunken, and held a distrustful, far-off stare. They were the eyes of a man who had thought long and hard, but always about the same things, and, like the man Dr. Johnson knew, he had wound up with only one idea and that a wrong one.

On this December Sunday evening in Rome—the year was 1941, and he was fifty-six years, one month, and one week old—he carried a typewritten sheaf of remarks on sundry matters, six or seven pages of them in his odd and loosely spaced typing style, which was full of abbreviations and punctuation of his own devising. They were notes for a talk, and he had come a long way to give it—all the way from Rapallo.

Although an American, he was no stranger at the Ente Italiano Audizione Radiofoniche, the government broadcasting agency. During the past year he had made a number of broadcasts intended to discourage British resistance. He had not been noticeably successful. He had also addressed himself to his countrymen, of whom he knew practically nothing, having lived abroad for thirty-three years with only a brief visit home in 1910 and a briefer one in 1939.

"You won't save democracy by stopping Italy's social reforms," he told them. Praising Mussolini's land reclamation program he said, "I don't think works like this should stop or that the war should be dragged on forever," and advised against giving aid to Britain, which would only drag it on. His wife was an English-woman; one wonders what she thought about it.

The State Department thought he should return home. On July 12 it had instructed the United States Embassy in Rome to limit his passport for immediate return, and it was extended for only six months to compel him to do so. Now, five months later, he was still in Italy, and about to give another talk.

His way of talking was just as odd as his way of typing. He spoke with many voices. In the midst of expositions in a flat, pedantic, and occasionally scolding tone, he would lapse into exaggerated Western drawls, Yankee twangings, feet-on-the-cracker-barrel pipings, and as suddenly switch to upper-class British sibilants and even Cockney growls. But while he looked and sometimes sounded like a mountebank, he was in deadly earnest.

At 6:12 P.M., Rome time, following the briefest of introductions—"We next present a talk by"—he took the announcer's place at the short-wave microphone. He began quietly, even casually, like one neighbor to another over the backyard fence. The typescript rattled in his hand unread. It was part of his skill to achieve, in a trice, a folksy, honest, open, and extemporaneous air.

"Europe calling. Pound speaking. Ezra Pound speaking, and I think I am perhaps still speaking a bit more to England than to the United States, but you folks may as well hear it. They say an Englishman's head is made of wood and the American head made of watermelon. Easier to get something into the American head but well-nigh impossible to make it stick there for ten minutes. Of course, I don't know what good I am doing, I mean what immediate good, but some things you folks on both sides of the wretched ocean will have to learn, war or no war, sooner or later."

The poet intruded.

"Now, what I had to say about the state of mind in England in 1919 I said in my *Cantos,* Cantos 14 and 15. Some of your philosophists and fancy thinkers would have called it the spiritual side of England. I undertake to say 'state of mind.' I can't say my remarks were heeded. I thought I got 'em simple enough."

He appealed to the happy few.

"I go on—try to make my meaning clear and then clearer—and in the long run people who listen to me, very few of 'em do, but the numbers of that small and select minority do know more in the long run than those who listen to, say, H. G. 'Chubby' Wells and the liberal stooges. What I'm gettin' at is, a friend said to me the other day that he was glad I had the politics I have got but that he didn't understand how I, as a North American United Stateser, could have it. Well, that looks simple to me. Things often do look simple to me."

The pedant intruded.

"On the Confucian system, very few start right and then go on—start at the roots and move upward. The pattern often is simple. Whereas, if you start constructing from the twig downward, you get into a muddle. My politics seem to me simple. My idea of a state or empire is more like a hedgehog or a porcupine—chunky and well-defended. I don't cotton to the idea of my country bein' an octopus, weak in the tentacles and suffering from stomach ulcers and colic gastritis."

He had the answer—along with Hitler, Himmler, and an unknown German in Rapallo.

"What I am ready to fight against is having ex-European Jews making another peace worse than Versailles with a new two dozen Danzigs."

He knew what had to be done.

"The sooner all America and all England wake up to what the war birds and Roosevelt are up to, the better for the next generation and this one."

England, however, was done for. He mocked the battered land.

"Ay, ay, sir, where is it? Did the [word or words missing owing to poor reception; in other places words are missing owing to transcriber's unfamiliarity with Pound's subject matter] King save it? He did not. Did the Goldschmitts save it? They did not. Does Churchill endeavor to save it? He does not. I repeat, the rot and stink of England and the danger to her empire are from the inside and have been from the time of [words missing; possibly a reference to the formation of the Bank of England in 1694], and no number of rabbis and bank clerks in Wall Street and in Washington can do one damn thing for England save to let her alone.

And a damn pity they didn't start doing so sooner. That is, a pity for England."

He knew where the blame lay.

"Roosevelt is more in the hands of the Jews than Wilson was in 1919."

He had written to President Wilson; more recently he had written to President Roosevelt about the nature of money and had sent him one of his books for further instruction.

"Eight years ago he was a-sayin' nothing to fear but fear. Well, what has become of that Roosevelt? What has he done for three years but try to work up a hysteria on that basis? He has got his face into a paper called 'Life,' eight or ten photographs. Why, Jim Farley would have been less nuisance in the White House than 'Snob' Delano, who objected to Farley, not on moral or ethical grounds, but purely as snobbism. Didn't want there to be a hench-man to succeed him."

The palaver poured forth; what was it but palaver? There was only one thing that Pound was really interested in, and he came to it near the end of his talk without transition—from Farley to finance.

"And as to American labor—when will American labor start looking into the currency question? Question—of course there oughtn't to be any interrogative element in it. Even a hod carrier ought to be able to learn why interest-paying debts is not so good a basis for money and its productive labor. Yes, but will they?"

It was "a corporate problem or issue" and he did not think the United States was quite ready to follow the example of Italy. "Lord knows I don't see how America can have Fascism without years of previous training." There was another way out. "Looks to me even now as if the currency problem was the place to start saving America, as I have been saying for some time back."

He had evolved a theory about economics which could never have been wholly clear to him, for he never was able to express it clearly; but upon his text, which appeared with variations, he had lavished volumes of exegesis, and he was to lavish many more. All the ills of mankind—all those, at least, since the age of craft guilds, of barter and usury, for he lived much in the past—could be ended, he thought, by his monetary scheme, which had come to him at second hand. He had the zeal and tirelessness of a reformer, and like many of that ilk could be harsh and vituperative. He promised to return to the subject.

The announcer: "And that was a talk by Ezra Pound entitled 'Those Parentheses.' This is the Italian Broadcasting System, transmitting the second daily program for North America."

It was 6:24 P.M., Rome time. In Washington, where the talk had been monitored by the Foreign Broadcast Intelligence Service of the Federal Communications Commission, it was 12:24 P.M., Eastern Standard Time.

-------------------------- 2 --------------------------

He walked with a swarming stride through the nightfall streets. Whether on the spur of the moment, or by plan, he had decided to call on two Americans he knew, Eleanor and Reynolds Packard, who were friendly and knowledgeable. There no longer was an American community in Rome; all who could had left the joyless wartime capital, which was blacked out and severely rationed. Packard was still there because of his job. He was the Rome correspondent for the United Press.

It was probably during this walk that Pound's status—his relation to other Americans as fixed by law—changed, although he did not know it. It had also changed in a more personal way, as regards the Packards, for example; this, too, he did not know, but was soon to find out.

Their first words came in a rush.

"The United States is at war!"

He saw the open suitcases.

In that tense confrontation was he aware of a new attitude toward him? Then it came. It was an accusation.

"If you stay," Packard said quietly, "you will be a traitor."

"I consider myself a 100 percent American and patriot," Pound retorted. Seeing the incredulous looks of the Packards, he added defensively: "I am only against Roosevelt and the Jews who influence him."

It was morning in Hawaii. The planes were burning on the flying fields of Honolulu, the battleships smoldered in the waters of Pearl Harbor.

--------------------------- **3** ---------------------------

Pound stayed.

Less than two months later—the United States was now at war with Germany and Italy as well as Japan—he was back on the air. He had taken a room at the Albergo d'Italia on the Via Giardini to be available for two—sometimes it was three—broadcasts a week on the Ente Italiano Audizione Radiofoniche's "American hour."

From what he afterward told his counsel it appears that he received an "advance" of 300 lire from the Ministry of Popular Culture of the Kingdom of Italy—i.e., Mussolini's corporate state— and an additional 350 lire after registering his script. Whether he was paid for all the broadcasts he made is problematical; by 1943, when Italy was invaded by both the Allies and the Germans—who took over the radio station on the Via Asiago—bookkeeping may have been difficult. Also, there were some broadcasts for which no payments were scheduled, for he sometimes spoke on programs other than his own, and was sometimes on the air when he did not know that he was.

As regards payments actually received, Pound told his counsel that the money barely covered his expenses, which included train fare and his hotel room. He told a reporter: "No German or Italian was ever in position to give me an order. So I took none. But a German near my home at Rapallo told me they were paying good money for broadcasts. That was a fatal mistake."

A German—not an Italian. It is a curious fact that much of what he said paralleled the Nazi propaganda line, not the Fascist. This was also true of home-grown Fascists in the United States.

The first of the new, consecutive series of talks took place January 29, 1942, at 9:30 P.M., EST, which meant that he got up in the middle of the night to deliver it. The brevity that had marked earlier introductions was a thing of the past; instead, an elaborately phrased preamble was offered by the announcer, who spoke respectfully in English. Plain Ezra Pound was metamorphosed into Dr. Ezra Pound, a prefix denoting academic rank which is highly regarded in Europe. To some of his listeners, however, who did not know who he was, or that he held several degrees, it meant nothing, or meant a medical doctor, a title which is even more highly regarded in the United States. The rest of the preamble appears to have been his answer to Packard's accusation, which probably rankled.

Announcer: "Rome Radio, acting in accordance with the Fascist policy of intellectual freedom and free expression of opinion by those who are qualified to hold it, has offered Dr. Ezra Pound the use of the microphone twice a week. It is understood that he will not be asked to say anything whatsoever that goes against his conscience, or anything incompatible with his duties as a citizen of the United States of America."

Dr. Pound: "Ezra Pound again speaking, speaking from Europe. Pearl Arbor Day, or Pearl Harbor Day, at twelve noon I retired from the capital of the old Roman Empire—that is, Rome—to Rapallo to seek wisdom from the ancients. I wanted to figure things out. I had a perfectly good alibi if I wanted to play things safe. I was and am officially occupied with a new translation of the [Odes?] of Confucius. I have in Rapallo the text of Confucius and of the [Analects?], and the text of the world's finest anthology, namely that which Confucius compiled from earlier authors."

He had also had a dictionary—"not the most up-to-date dictionary of Chinese ideograms, but nevertheless good enough." He praised the ideograms.

"They are of extreme beauty. Thousands of poets have looked at those hills and despaired. There are points at which some simple ideogram, that is, the Chinese picture world, is so used, to its [ultimate expression that it reaches as?] far as our human sense of eternity can reach. There is one of the sunrise that I despair of ever getting change to meet it. There was to be [however, a change in my?] situation.

"That is to say, the United States has been for months [words missing] and illegally at war through what I considered to be the criminal acts of a President whose mental condition was not, so far as I could see, all that could or should be desired of a man in so responsible a position or office. He has, so far as the evidence to me available showed, broken his promises to his electorate. He had to my mind violated his oath of office. He had to my mind violated the oath of allegiance to the United States Constitution which even the ordinary citizen is expected to take every time he gets a new passport. It was obviously a mere question of hours between that day and time when the United States would be legally at war with the Axis.

"I spent a month trying to figure things out. Well, did I? Perhaps I concluded sooner. At any rate I had a month clear to make up my mind about some things. I had Confucius and [Aristotle?], both of whom had been up against similar problems, both of whom had seen empires fallen, both of whom had seen deeper into the causes of human confusion than most men ever think of [or] are looking for."

His father, Homer Loomis Pound, was living in Rapallo, in an apartment formerly occupied by William Butler Yeats. Enter palaver.

"And then there was my old dad in bed with a broken hip. Lord knows who's going to mend it or when it is going to mend. So I read him a few pages of Aristotle in the [Loeb] Classical Library as diversion to take his mind off it. Also to keep my own work-in-progress progressing; and because for some time I had in mind the need of comparing the terminology of the Chinese and Greek philosophy and comparing that to the terminology of medieval Catholic theology."

Exit preamble.

"The United States has been misinformed. The United States has been led down the garden path and maybe down under the daisies. All through shutting out news."

Enter Jews.

"There is no end to the amount of shutting out news that the sons of [word or name missing: perhaps Isaac or Abraham] who started this war and wanted this war and monkeyed around to keep the war going and spreading, there is no end to the shutting out, the perversions of news, that these blighters ain't up to."

His sources of information were purer. Vice President Wallace was "telling the world that there would be no peace till the nations of the world knuckled under and bowed down to the gold standard." (The United States had gone off the gold standard in 1933.) The "London gold ring" was asking Britons "to go out and die for gold." (Great Britain, which went off the gold standard in 1931, had returned to it under Churchill. The economist John Maynard Keynes thought Churchill wrong on this, and, the Prime Minister later concurred. But Keynes was also excoriated by Pound.)

"Yes, I knew that this was what the war was about; I knew the war was about gold, usury, and monopoly. I said as much when I was last in America. I then said, 'if the war is pushed on us.' So now the United States has got pushed out of Guam and Wake, and I suppose out of the Philippines, and a Thirty Years' War is in progress. Is it? Is a Thirty Years' War what the American citizen thinks will do most good to the United States of America?

"Or has somebody been misinformed? And if so, who misinformed him? According to the reports of the American press now available to the average European, someone in charge of American destiny miscalculated something or other. We hear that an inquiry is in progress, it being my private belief that I could have avoided the war with Japan if anyone had the unlikely idea of sending me out there with any thought of official powers."

He attacked a BBC commentator for "telling his presumably music-hall audience that the 'Japs' were jackals. And that they had recently—I think he said within living man's lifetime—emerged from barbarism." He listed some of the Noh plays, which he had translated from the manuscripts and notes of Ernest Fenollosa, the American who became Imperial Commissioner of Arts in Japan. "These are Japanese classical plays, would convince any man with more sense than a peahen of the degree of Japanese civilization.

Let alone what they conserved when China was and [continued to be?] incapable of preserving her own cultural heritage. China letting Confucius go out of the schools, for example."

He deplored the alliance with Russia. President Roosevelt had no right "to dictate the citizen's politics." England was most to blame. He gave as his own the official German view:

"The day Hitler went into Russia, England had her chance to pull out. She had her chance to say 'Let bygones be bygones. If you stop this Muscovite order, we will let bygones be bygones. We will try to see at least half of your argument.' Instead of which Hank Wallace comes up saying no peace till the world accepts the gold standard [words missing]. Whom God would destroy He first sends to the bughouse."

two

The Poet

————————————— 1 —————————————

"I don't have to try *to be American. Merrymount, Braintree,
Quincy, all I believe in or by; what had been 'a plantation named
Weston's.' Vide also the host in Longfellow's 'Wayside Inn.' Wall
ornament there mentioned still at my parents'."*
—POUND, in a letter, 1939

Ezra Pound was born October 30, 1885, in the first plastered house
in Hailey, Territory of Idaho. His father was Homer Loomis
Pound, recorder, by appointment of President Arthur, of the
government land office there. His mother was Isabel Weston
Pound, a distant relation of Henry Wadsworth Longfellow
(through Joseph Wadsworth, who stole the Connecticut charter
and hid it in "Charter Oak"). He was an only child.

14

Pound has variously signed himself Ezra Weston Pound, Ezra Weston Loomis Pound and, what appears to be his preference, Ezra Loomis Pound. That preference may be explained by admiration for his Loomis ancestors, many of whom fought in the Revolution, and some of whom became notorious in upstate New York as "the Loomis Gang." They were "very good horse-thieves, never, I think, brought to book," Pound has commented. The state legislature investigated them, but did nothing. They were "brought to book" by a posse, with shootings, hangings, and barn burnings, but the Loomis women, who were much admired, were not molested. Two of them married into the Pound family.

Pound's paternal grandfather, who married Angevine Loomis, was Thaddeus Coleman Pound, a lumberman, lieutenant-governor of Wisconsin, and a member of Congress. A contemporary account credits him with "merchandizing in about all of its branches, agriculture in all its forms." His company issued its own scrip:

STATE OF WISCONSIN
Union Lumbering Company
Chippewa Falls
Will pay to the bearer on demand
FIFTY CENTS
IN MERCHANDISE OR LUMBER

Thaddeus Pound built railroads in Wisconsin and owned silver mines in the Territory of Idaho. In that period of "jumped claims" a government land office was essential; Homer Pound opened one in Hailey (altitude: 5,342 feet) and became an expert assayer as well. He brought his bride there after a honeymoon at Niagara Falls and Chippewa Falls. She did not like the altitude. Her mother did not like the unlocked doors.

"Oh! Homer, how could you bring my daughter to *such* a place?"

"Lock! Lock! You wouldn't, a man wouldn't, lock his door out there," Homer Pound told his son later. "If you locked your door, they'd suspicion you."

The altitude was decisive. At eighteen months Ezra Pound was brought east by his parents, who settled first in Philadelphia, where Homer Pound became assistant assayer of the United States Mint, and afterward in Wyncote, a suburb, where the boy grew up.

He was not quite sixteen when he entered the University of Pennsylvania where a fellow student was William Carlos Williams. A year after their meeting, Williams wrote his mother to tell her about his weekend visit in Wyncote:

"After supper Pound and I went to his room where we had a long talk on subjects that I love yet have not time to study and which he is making a life work of. That is literature, and the drama and the classics, also a little philosophy. He, Pound, is a fine fellow; he is the essence of optimism and has a cast-iron faith that is something to admire. If ever he gets blue nobody knows it, so he is just the man for me. But not one person in a thousand likes him, and a great many people detest him and why? Because he is so darned full of conceits and affectation."

After two years at Penn, Pound switched to Hamilton College, in Clinton, New York, a region where the Loomis Gang had operated. His favorite garb was a scarlet turtleneck sweater. He was graduated in 1905, and returned to the University of Pennsylvania for postgraduate work, winning a fellowship in Romanics, which gave him a year abroad. For his doctor's thesis he pursued his studies of Lope de Vega in the royal library in Madrid; later he went to Burgos, where he found the remains of the house of one of his heroes—El Cid. He also wrote an article about the city— "Burgos: A Dream City of Old Castile"—which appeared in the October, 1906, issue of *The Book News Monthly,* a publication of the John Wanamaker Store in Philadelphia.

A teaching career was open to him when he returned. He accepted a post at Wabash College, Crawfordsville, Indiana, but was dismissed after four months. He afterward noted that "all accusations" were "ultimately refuted save that of being 'the Latin Quarter type.'" A shocked landlady had found a woman in his room.

The night before, at a late hour, he had gone out to mail a letter. It was snowing hard. He encountered a young woman from a stranded burlesque show—cold, hungry, and with no place to sleep. He fed her and gave her his bed; he himself slept on the floor. The year was 1907; Pound was engaged to a Miss Mary Moore, and was in fact searching for living quarters for himself and his bride-to-be when the dismissal occurred. The letter was to her.

The engagement, but not their friendship, ended soon after. The book that brought him fame was dedicated to her; six decades later the enlarged edition of *Personae,* which contains his collected poems, still bears that dedication:

THIS BOOK IS FOR
MARY MOORE
OF TRENTON, IF SHE
WANTS IT

Wabash College paid up on its contract, which was for a year. One of the students there was Thurman Arnold, the Washington attorney who represented Pound in the final disposition of his case in 1958.

With academic circles seemingly closed to him, Pound went abroad again in 1908. He appears to have felt keenly the fact that the University of Pennsylvania, where he had gained his M.A. and at whose graduate school he had done important research, did not offer him a job. Twenty-one years later the alumni secretary wrote him to solicit funds. Pound wrote back: "All the U. of P. or your damn college or any other god damn American college does or will do for a man of letters is to ask him to go away without breaking the silence."

2

He was twenty-three years old. Even before he grew the long mustache and the thin, pointed beard his appearance was remarkable. He was tall, slender, and powerfully knit from fencing and tennis, two sports he was proficient in and which he was to keep up. There were also, of course, the red-gold hair, the green eyes, the straight nose, and the cleft and stubborn chin.

Inside him, there was something equally remarkable: a generous nature that is perhaps unique in the annals of literature. His gifts and energies were at the beck and call and service of others, provided only that these others were creative. At such times his own work and ambitions became secondary. His enthusiasms pulled him this way and that, but they pushed others to the top.

He went to Venice, where for the first time he all but gave up his career. He became the friend and impresario of a pianist whose specialty was Scriabin. He arranged a "press conference" for her. He wrote to a friend in the United States to help line up recitals. He wrote to the Paris *Herald,* in a letter mailed from Venice and signed "E. P.":

"Katherine Ruth Heyman, whose American tournee is predicted as the event of the coming piano season there, may give certain concerts in Paris on her way West.

"Her playing in London before sailing is also to be announced."

He accompanied Miss Heyman to London, where their paths diverged.

London had been his real goal from the start. He hoped to meet Yeats, whom he greatly admired (he even wore pince-nez because Yeats did). A flat at No. 10 Church Walk, Kensington, became his home for several years. His was a precarious existence. He wrote his friend Williams in October, 1908: "My days of utter privation are over for a space." He had found a job lecturing on "Developments of Literature in Southern Europe" at the Regent Street branch of the Polytechnic Institute. The following year his course was entitled "Medieval Literature." Between terms he published *Personae.*

He wrote Mary Moore, with whom he was in constant correspondence: "Is London fun? Sometimes. Six months ago it was decidedly not." Now he was meeting everyone. He lunched with Laurence Binyon, with Maurice Hewlett; had tea with May Sinclair; attended a Poets Club dinner, where he heard Shaw speak; went to suppers at the home of Ernest Rhys, an original member of the Rhymers' Club of the Nineties—at one of these, when Yeats was also present, Ford Madox Ford brought D. H. Lawrence. "In other words I am beginning to get acquainted with the interesting part of London & it is pretty much fun."

He ordered a "directoire overcoat."

Williams came to see him. Pound's room struck him as very small. "You could touch all the walls standing in the middle of it." He discovered that his friend "was very much in love with someone whose picture he kept on his dresser, with a candle perpetually lighted before it. He never explained who she was."

"He really lived the poet as few of us had the nerve to live that exalted reality in our time," Williams afterward recalled.

He wore a coat with blue glass buttons, a black velvet jacket, one turquoise earring. He asked a hostess: "Why do you give us solid stuff like roast beef and plum pudding for lunch?" He asked the company: "Would you like to see how an American eats an apple?" and proceeded to quarter his and gobble it. Once, after refusing all offers of food, he dismembered a rose and munched the petals; finding them to his liking, he reached for another. Unfortunately for him, when he rose from the table he washed his ethereal meal down with a carafe of water, taken at a gulp; reclining himself on a sofa, he gurgled "interminably" all evening.

At a meeting of poets, after the others had quietly read their latest effusions, he rose and declaimed "Sestina: Altaforte," an adaptation from Bertran de Born, a troubadour poet; it begins, "Damn it all! all this our South stinks peace." Pound's way of reading it was superb; the only trouble was it took place in a Soho restaurant. Everything stopped—waiters in their tracks, uplifted forks twined with spaghetti.

3

It was on April 16, 1909, that *Personae of Ezra Pound* appeared —a slender volume of fifty-nine pages bound in brown boards stamped with gold lettering, and bearing the durable dedication. It sold for six shillings sixpence. The publisher, who was also a bookseller, had a shop on Vigo Street, off Regent.

There are several amusing versions of the way in which the book was accepted; Pound's own account of "that touching little scene in Elkins Mathews' shop" occurs in a letter.

"Mathews: 'Ah, eh, ah, would you, now, be prepared to assist in the publication?'

"E. P.: 'I've a shilling in my clothes, if that's any use to you.'

"Mathews: 'Oh well, I want to publish 'em. Anyhow.' "

The reviews of *Personae* must have been gratifying. The *Observer* wrote: "Criticism and praise alike give no idea of it." The *Daily Chronicle:* "It is the old miracle that cannot be defined, nothing more than a subtle entanglement of words, so that they rise out of their graves and sing." *Punch* observed that "Mr. Ezekiel Ton" was "by far the newest poet going, whatever other advertisements may say."

Other volumes of verse, as well as translations and critical studies, followed. Pound's poems showed an enormous originality and range; many have withstood the changing tastes of six decades. His work inspired other poets and helped to shape their styles. He is not only inseparable from the history of modern British and American poetry; in large part he is that history.

In 1912 Harriet Monroe, founder and first editor of *Poetry: A Magazine of Verse,* wrote him from Chicago for advice and help. He replied: "Can you teach the American poet that poetry *is* an *art,* an art with a technique, with media—an art that must be in constant flux, a constant change of manner, if it is to live?" A half century and five years later his next question rings clearer than ever: "Can you teach him that it is not a pentametric echo of the sociological dogma printed in last year's magazines?"

He agreed to publish exclusively in *Poetry,* and to send the work of others. When he got around to sending his own work, he wrote: "You must use your own discretion about printing this batch of verses. At any rate, don't use them until you've used 'H. D.' and Aldington." He contributed the first review to appear in the United States of Robert Frost's first book, published in

London. He also sent poems by three future Nobel laureates: William Butler Yeats, "to set the tone"; Rabindranath Tagore—"he has sung Bengal into a nation"; and T. S. Eliot. Miss Monroe gave him a hard time over Eliot, but he finally persuaded her.

Yeats and Pound had become close friends. The recollections of many who attended Yeats's famous "Mondays" indicate that Pound was always there. One of the guests was astonished at the way in which Pound dominated the company, distributing Yeats's cigarettes and Chianti, and "laying down the law" about poetry. A Yeats biographer states that the older poet's life in Woburn Buildings, in the winter of 1912–1913, "was only rendered tolerable by the assiduous attentions of Pound," who also gave Yeats fencing lessons.

In the winter of 1913 Pound became Yeats's secretary. Whatever he may have learned from this association, the record is clear that Yeats learned a great deal from Pound. Yeats wrote to Lady Gregory: "He is full of the Middle Ages and helps me to get back to the definite and concrete." But in a letter to Sir William Rothenstein he complained that Pound had "a rugged and headstrong nature, and he is always hurting people's feelings."

Pound had got used to "laying down the law" about poetry. But was this the way to do it? Phyllis Bottome recalled: "He spoke in short staccato sentences like the bark of an angry dog. He wore his brain outside of him like a skin; and that terrific exposure made him always vulnerable and hostile." Sir Osbert Sitwell wrote: "He was particularly a type the English do not understand or appreciate."

Richard Aldington summarized: "Ezra started out in a time of peace and prosperity with everything in his favor, and muffed his chances of becoming literary dictator of London—to which he undoubtedly aspired—by his own conceit, folly and bad manners. Eliot started in the enormous confusion of war and post-war England, handicapped in every way. Yet by merit, tact, prudence, and pertinacity he succeeded in doing what no other American has ever done—imposing his personality, taste, and even many of his opinions on literary England."

On the other hand, other witnesses testified differently.

Douglas Goldring: "I was a bit suspicious of Ezra at first, and, though I am rather ashamed to admit it, perhaps a trifle jealous of him. . . . But one day I happened to see round Ezra's pince-nez, and noticed that he had curiously kind, affectionate eyes. This chance discovery altered my whole conception of him. Perhaps it reveals part of the secret of his hold over Ford. Ezra could be a friend, and not merely a fair-weather one."

Violet Hunt, Ford's mistress: "Ezra, a dear, lived near us, and was in and out all day. He was very kind to the editor [of *The English Review:* Ford], and would do any sort of job for him or me, using up his intense and feverish energy in taking down winged words at dictation, or tying up my creeper for me." The creeper was in her garden on Campden Hill, where Pound played tennis with Ford, Hugh Walpole, and others, "like a demon or a trick pony, sitting down composedly in his square and jumping up in time to receive his adversary's ball, which he competently returned."

John Cournos: "The salient impression I received as I watched him across the table in the public house was that of almost exuberant kindness. And Ezra, as I had cause to find out, was one of the kindest men that ever lived."

Cournos "inherited" the little room at 10 Church Walk when Pound married and moved to a flat around the corner.

4

Pound's bride was Dorothy Shakespear, the daughter of Henry Hope Shakespear, a London solicitor. Her mother, Olivia, was a friend of Yeats, and appears in one of his poems. The marriage took place in St. Mary Abbot's, the parish church of Kensington, on Monday, April 20, 1914. Pound was twenty-eight, his wife twenty-seven. Eliot has described their "small dark flat" at No. 5 Holland Place Chambers, where Pound did the cooking by artificial light, and worked and received visitors in a small room which was "inconveniently triangular."

Pound gave Eliot the impression of "being only a temporary squatter. This appearance was due, not only to his restless energy—in which it was difficult to distinguish the energy from the restlessness and the fidgets, so that every room, even a big one, seemed too small for him—but to a kind of resistance to growing into any environment. In America, he would no doubt have always seemed on the point of going abroad; in London, he always seemed on the point of crossing the Channel."

Pound crossed the Channel a number of times before settling in Paris with his wife in 1921. There, as in Kensington, a new and brilliant group of writers attached themselves to him, including Ernest Hemingway. "Ezra Pound was always a good friend and he was always doing things for people," Hemingway wrote later. In his courtyard studio on the rue Notre Dame des Champs he cut and edited the manuscript of *The Waste Land,* which was published in the form in which he left it. And, having earlier found James Joyce a publisher and patron in England, he now brought the author of *A Portrait of the Artist As a Young Man* from Zürich to Paris, where *Ulysses* was completed.

He championed the American composer George Antheil, got him a concert hall, saw the performance of "Ballet Mécanique" crowned with success despite organized rowdyism, and afterward wrote a book entitled *Antheil and the Treatise on Harmony* to find the composer a larger audience. Earlier, he had written a book about a young sculptor friend, Gaudier-Brzeska, killed in World War I.

"Gertrude Stein liked him," she or Miss Toklas wrote in *The Autobiography of Alice B. Toklas,* "but did not find him amusing. She said he was a village explainer, excellent if you were a village, but if you were not, not."

Malcolm Cowley called on him when Hemingway was present; Pound did all the talking—Hemingway listened "as if with his eyes." They made a date for tennis, and Hemingway left. Pound began to give Cowley "the lowdown on the Elizabethan drama." Exhibiting a leather-bound folio, he said: "The whole business is cribbed from these Italian state papers." He had already put some of them into the *Cantos.* It was time for him to stop helping others, he said—he had the *Cantos* to finish, an opera he wanted to write. Perhaps he would leave Paris for Italy.

Pound's reasons for leaving England are unclear. He had missed the experience of the war which his friends had shared, even Cournos, who was an American and who had served Britain in a civilian capacity. Aldington, finding Pound "violently hostile to England," instantly thought he meant that he had been menaced by returning troops as a slacker." But "it eventually came out that he was implying that the English had no brains."

For this bizarre conclusion two explanations are possible.

"Hugh Selwyn Mauberley" (read: Ezra Loomis Pound), a sequence which consists of eighteen short poems, and which is his masterpiece, reflects among other things his disillusionment with the "botched civilization" revealed by World War I and disappointment with his own place as a poet, perhaps even his role socially. The following note occurs before "Mauberley" in the enlarged *Personae:* "The sequence is so distinctly a farewell to London that the reader who chooses to regard this as an exclusively American edition may as well omit it and turn at once to page 205" (the poem occupies pp. 185–204).

Thus far the poet.

Money, or the lack of it, could never have been far from his thoughts. It became, at length, an obsession, which he expressed in political as well as economic terms. He had met others besides writers and artists.

Alfred Richard Orage was the editor of *The New Age,* to which Pound had contributed (he was also its music and art critic). Orage was a Guild Socialist with visions of a better world, an anti-Semitic one. He introduced Pound to Major C. H. Douglas, the "inventor" or "apostle" of Social Credit. Major Douglas had some elementary ideas about finance—*viz.,* the "real" credit of a nation resides in a people's capacity to produce needed goods, but "money" had been "cornered," so that "financial credit" controlled "real" credit. Who had done the cornering? Alas.

Pound reviewed their books. His *Cantos* began to reflect their simplifications, anti-Semitism—and something else: he had found a cause.

From this point on we are confronted by a dual personality: the poet and defender of poets and artists, and a man of coarse speech and muddled mind lit by fierce hatreds.

Cantos XIV and XV, to which he referred in his Pearl Harbor Day broadcast, are all but unprintable (the following extract is given as published):

> The stench of wet coal, politicians
> . . . . .e and . . . . . n, their wrists bound to
> their ankles,
> Standing bare bum,
> Faces smeared on their rumps,
> wide eye on flat buttock,
> Bush hanging for beard,
> Addressing crowds through their arse-holes,
> Addressing the multitudes in the ooze,
> newts, water-slugs, water-maggots,
> And with them . . . . r,
> a scrupulously clean table-napkin
> Tucked under his penis,
> and . . . . m
> Who disliked colloquial language,
> Stiff-starched, but soiled, collars
> circumscribing his legs,
> The pimply and hairy skin
> pushing over the collar's edge,
> Profiteers drinking blood sweetened with sh-t,
> And behind them . . . . . . f and the financiers
> lashing them with steel wires.

Who would know from all this that he was lashing the monopolists, the obstructors of knowledge, and the obstructors of distribution, except that he says so at the close of Canto XIV? Canto XV is more of the same. Thus the reformer on "the spiritual side of England," which had bled to death on the Somme, as Pound conceived it in 1919.

three

The Antithetical Self

———————— 1 ————————

Paris was left behind in 1925. After some shuttlings to and fro—
Florence, Assisi, Rome, Taormina, Siracusa, Palermo—Pound and
his wife settled in Rapallo, No. 12, Via Marsala, five flights up.
There was a terrace; Gaudier-Brzeska's monumental head of the
poet, weathering these many years in Violet Hunt's garden in
Kensington, arrived and was set up at one end of it. The workroom
—his desk was next to a French window which opened on the
terrace—was strung with cords to which were attached envelopes
and manuscript pages, his "active" filing system Pound liked to
term it. When he went out for his constitutional he donned a cape
and a broad-brimmed hat with which he saluted other promen-
aders on the *lungomare,* Cavalier style, with a swoop and sweep.

He had found, at last, an environment into which to grow.

"I personally think extremely well of Mussolini," he wrote

Harriet Monroe. "If one compares him to American presidents (the last three) or British premiers, etc., in fact one can NOT without insulting him. If the intelligentsia don't think well of him, it is because they know nothing about 'the state,' and government, and have no particularly large sense of values. Anyhow, WHAT intelligentsia?"

William Butler Yeats came to live in Rapallo. The two poets were now related—Yeats had married, in 1917, Miss Georgie Hyde-Lees, the stepdaughter of Olivia Shakespear's brother. Yeats wrote Mrs. Shakespear: "Ezra and Dorothy seem happy and content, pleased with their way of life, and Dorothy and [Georgie] compare their experience of infancy and its strange behavior."

The Pounds had a son, born 1926 in the American hospital in Paris. He was named Omar Shakespear Pound; Mrs. Shakespear told John Cournos that Pound had reeled off the names of her grandson and then exclaimed, "Just note the crescendo!"

To Yeats, Rapallo, on the Ligurian Sea below Genoa, was "an incredibly lovely place"—he thought it might even be the little town described in Keats's "Ode on a Grecian Urn." He hoped to find rest: "Here I shall put off the bitterness of Irish quarrels." When his health permitted, he resumed the fencing lessons in the workroom hung with manuscripts and correspondence.

Richard Aldington came to Rapallo. He found Pound, who entertained him at his tennis club, "his usual genial and modest self." Despite his various critical remarks, Aldington quite often defended Pound. He did so when he had Yeats and his wife to dinner. Yeats asked him: "How do you account for Ezra?"

This was beyond Aldington's powers.

"Here is a man," Yeats resumed, "who produces the most distinguished work and yet in his behavior is the least distinguished of men. It is the antithetical self."

Aldington ventured to suggest that "all this throwing down of fire-irons and sputtering of four-letter words is merely Ezra's form of defense against a none too considerate world."

Aldington left, and Yeats continued to bear the brunt. He wrote Lady Gregory: 'I see Ezra daily. We disagree about everything." He was not displeased when Wyndham Lewis attacked Pound in

Time and Western Man as "the revolutionary simpleton." It now struck him that there was a resemblance between Pound and the Irish rebel he had loved in his youth; Pound, he told Lady Gregory, "has most of Maud Gonne's opinions (political and economic) about the world in general." More: "He has even her passion for cats."

The cats waited for Pound at a street corner every night, when he fed great numbers. "Anyone *must* like Ezra, who has seen him feeding the stray cats of Rapallo," Yeats told Sir Osbert Sitwell. He kept on trying. When he and his wife left Rapallo, their apartment on the Via Americhe was taken by Pound's parents. Sir Max Beerbohm, who lived in Rapallo and had met Pound several times, now met them. He told S. N. Behrman: "He idolized them, and they idolized him." The walls were adorned with photographs of Ezra from childhood on.

In 1930 Pound and his wife went to London, where they left Omar with his maternal grandmother; on the way back to Italy they stopped off in Paris to visit Ford Madox Ford. A woman who was present at the dinner Ford gave them in his apartment on the rue de Vaugirard described Pound as "a very large man, very American, talking like an American, somewhat pompous." Despite his strenuous tennis and fencing, and rowing far out on a *pontone* in order to swim alone, he was putting on weight. Dorothy Pound was "absolutely beautiful, beautiful with authentic beauty. She was very fair, with blue eyes, the most unadorned woman I've ever seen—no lipstick, no make-up, hair merely drawn back."

Pound published that year *A Draft of XXX Cantos*, and the following year one of his masterpieces of translation. Dr. E. A. Lowe, the world-renowned paleographer, has recounted a meeting with him in the Vatican Library.

"One day, while ordering a manuscript," he recalled, "I noticed that the slip made out before mine was signed Ezra Pound. I asked who wrote that slip and a man with a small beard and italianate cloak was pointed out to me.

"In due time I walked up behind him and whispered the words, 'What's a poet doing in the Vatican?' He simply turned his head to me and whispered back, 'Shall we have lunch?' He was, in fact, working on his edition of Guido Cavalcanti.

"I enjoyed the lunch and the tea the next day when I met his wife, and in time I paid two visits to Rapallo."

Guido Cavalcanti: Rime was published in Genoa, Edizioni Marsano, "Anno IX."

2

Pound's letters, postcards, even his books, were now invariably dated Fascist style, from the "March on Rome" in 1922. His letterhead bore a drawing of him by Gaudier-Brzeska and a motto by Mussolini: "Liberty is a duty not a right." He met Mussolini for the first and only time in 1933, as recorded in Canto XLI, where he terms him "the Boss." The occasion appears to have been the presentation of a copy of *A Draft of XXX Cantos;* Mussolini was amused—"è divertente."

In the same Canto he praised Mussolini's land reclamation program, the draining of the marshes "XI of our era," in the belief that it had not been done before.

He wrote Professor J. H. Rogers, a member of President Roosevelt's Brain Trust in London for a conference ("18 Sept Anno XI"): "I don't care what you DO, so long as it isn't on my conscience that you are an Abroaded innocent/trusting in British vipers, Genevan mandrakes, and ignorant of Douglas, and ras moneta (stamp scrip)."

He wrote on a postcard to Roosevelt: "Lest you forget the nature of money/i;e; that it is a ticket. For the govt. To issue it against any particular merchandise or metal, is merely to favor the owners of that metal and by just that much to betray the rest of the public. You can see that the bill here photod. has SERVED (I mean by the worn state of the note). Certificates of work done. That is what these notes were in fact/ before the bank swine got the monopoly."

The front of the postcard showed a reproduction of the fifty-cent scrip issued by the Union Lumbering Company, Chippewa Falls, Wisconsin. It had served in Grandfather Pound's stores for Grandfather Pound's merchandise.

In Canto XLIV he wrote:

> and June 28th came men of Arezzo
> past the Porta Romana and went into the ghetto
> there to sack and burn hebrews
> part were burned with the liberty tree in the piazza
> and for the rest of that day and night
> 1799 anno domini

They were all usurers. (Sack: plunder.)

His views on money poured forth to premiers, cabinet ministers, senators, congressmen, bankers, economists, editors and journalists, and to anyone who ventured to write to him. A young poet in Wyncote, who worshiped him, sent some verses and received in reply a harsh admonition to study economics.

For one who had preached so much about the poet's art and disciplines, Pound had indeed begun to appear antithetical. The four-letter words were written as well as sputtered. He had set out to reform the world, and like all reformers he was dogmatic and impatient.

He was also erratic.

In his sixty-ninth year, William Butler Yeats, the greatest poet of the twentieth century, returned unexpectedly to Rapallo. He had not written any verse for two years; now, with all but one of the lyrics for *The King of the Great Clock Tower* done, doubts assailed him. He decided, as he afterward confessed, "to get the advice of a poet not of my school who would, as he did some years ago, say what he thought."

He asked Pound to dine with him, and waited for a request to read what he had written. It did not come. Pound would not talk about literature.

"He said, apropos of nothing 'Arthur Balfour was a scoundrel' and from that on would talk of nothing but politics. All the modern statesmen were more or less scoundrels except 'Mussolini and that hysterical imitator of him Hitler.'"

Yeats objected to Pound's "violence," but Pound, continuing in the same vein, urged him to read the works of Major Douglas, "who alone knew what caused our suffering." Yeats said that for him detective stories and stories of the Wild West sufficed as pictures of modern life; for serious reading, he had returned to Shakespeare and planned to go on to Chaucer. Pound merely denounced Dublin as "a reactionary hole."

He was prevailed on to take the manuscript with him. The next day he left it at Yeats's hotel. Scrawled across the first page was a single word: "Putrid."

----------------------------- **3** -----------------------------

From time to time Pound made serious efforts to formalize his monetary views. *Ezra Pound's ABC of Economics* is one of them; the *Money Pamphlets by £* were others. In the *ABC* he wrote:

"There are four elements; and it is useless trying to function with three:

"1. The product.

"2. The want.

"3. The means of transport.

"4. AND the certificates of value, preferably legal tender and 'general,' in the sense that they should be good for wheat, iron, lumber, dress goods or whatever the heart and stomach desire."

Who would run things (including the printing presses)?

"The brains of the nation or group to be used in discerning WHAT work is most needful, what work is less necessary and what is desirable even though not strictly necessary."

A postscript to the book is signed "E. P. Feb. 12, anno XI dell' era Fascista"—that is, Lincoln's Birthday, in the eleventh year of the Fascist era, 1933.

In the thirteenth year of the Fascist era he published a book entitled *Jefferson and/or Mussolini*. The title? "The fundamental likenesses between these two men are probably greater than their differences." Jefferson had made things. "I don't believe any estimate of Mussolini will be valid unless it starts from his passion for construction." Pound sent a copy to President Roosevelt.

In the same year he began the series of *Money Pamphlets* with *An Introduction to the Economic Nature of the United States,* written in Italian, as were the second, fourth, and sixth. The other titles are:

Gold and Work, What Is Money For?, A Visiting Card, Social Credit: An Impact, America, Roosevelt and the Causes of the Present War. (This was published in 1944.)

Pound wrote in the first: "The true history of the economy of the United States, as I see it, is to be found in the correspondence between Adams and Jefferson, in the writings of Van Buren, and in quotations from the intimate letters of the Fathers of the Republic," from which he quotes copiously in the *Cantos.* "The elements remain the same: debts, altering the value of monetary units, and the attempts, and triumphs of usury, due to monopolies, or to a 'Corner.' "

By the time he wrote the third—*What Is Money For?*—he had become interested in Silvio Gesell's theory of the velocity of money circulation, or Schwundgeld—"shrinking money"—which was not only taxed if not used by a stated time, but lost part of its value. He even journeyed to a place where it, or something like it, had been tried out—Wörgl, in the Austrian Tyrol, a place, he afterward wrote, which had "sent shivers down the backs of all the lice of Europe, Rothschildian and others."

It was in the third that he included his "Introductory Text Book," which follows in its entirety:

Chapter I

All the perplexities, confusion, and distress in America arise, not from defects in their Constitution or confederation, not from want of honor or virtue, so much as from downright ignorance of the nature of coin, credit, and circulation.

JOHN ADAMS

Chapter II

. . . and if the national bills issued be bottomed (as is indispensable) on pledges of specific taxes for their redemption within certain and moderate epochs, and be of proper denominations for circulation, no interest on them would be necessary or just, because they would answer to every one of the purposes of the metallic money withdrawn and replaced by them.

THOMAS JEFFERSON (*Letter to Crawford, 1816*)

Chapter III

. . . and gave the people of this Republic the greatest blessing they ever had—their own paper to pay their own debts.

ABRAHAM LINCOLN

Chapter IV

The Congress shall have Power . . .

To coin Money, regulate the Value thereof, and of foreign Coin, and to fix the Standard of Weights and Measures.

Constitution of the United States, Article I

Legislative Department, Section 8, clause 5

done in Convention by the Unanimous Consent of the States present the Seventeenth Day of September in the Year of our Lord one thousand seven hundred and Eighty-seven and of the Independence of the United States of America the Twelfth. In Witness whereof We have hereunto subscribed our Names.

GEORGE WASHINGTON—*President and Deputy from Virginia*

This is the way he reconciled Social Credit and Schwundgeld: "Douglas' proposals are a sub-head under the main idea in Lincoln's sentence, Gesell's 'invention' is a special case under Jefferson's general law."

He liked the "Introductory Text Book" so much that he repeated it in the sixth pamphlet with the following commentary:

"Lincoln was assassinated after he made the statement given above.

"The theatrical gesture of the assassin does not explain how it happened that he escaped from Washington, after the alarm had been raised, by the *only* road that was not guarded; nor its synchronization with the attempted assassination of Seward, the Secretary of State, nor various other details of the affair. The fact remains that Lincoln had assumed a position in clear opposition to the usurocracy."

He had already printed the "Text Book" separately, to facilitate mailing it. It is conceivable that the Rapallo post office handled more letters by Pound than by anyone else. Major Douglas complained from London: "Pending engaging a whole-time secretary to correspond with you I suggest that you concentrate on the subject of taxation as a form of modern highway robbery combined with iniquitous interference with the freedom of the individual."

—————————— **4** ——————————

A young poet came to Rapallo. He was Louis Zukofsky, in the very forefront of the New York avant-garde, much admired by Pound, who had sent him part of his passage money. Zukofsky was quartered with Pound's parents, with whom he breakfasted. He had tea every day with Ezra Pound, who, he observed, consumed great quantities of Italian pastry. His other meals, for which Pound paid, were taken with the poet Basil Bunting and his family. Between the breakfasts and the teas, Pound tried to convert Zukofsky to Social Credit. So did his father at breakfast. Both failed.

Back in New York, Zukofsky sent a poetry manuscript. Pound commented: "The next anthology will be econ/conscious and L/Z won't be in it." His father wrote: "Ezra had me read your book of poems and I must confess that it seems to me you could spend your time and talents on a much more needed Message to the world. Put your book aside, take up Social Credit, get in touch with 'New Democracy 55-5th Ave. New York." His letterhead also had a motto, his own: "Leisure Spare Time Free From Anxiety."

The correspondence between Pound and Zukofsky continued for several years. There are enough of Pound's letters to the younger man to make a book—an abusive one. Zukofsky, while conciliatory, could also be sharp in his rejoinders:

"No one in the U.S.A. is interested in the Boss's reclamations of the marshes—& quite a number here are aware of the fact that Rome when it was caving in did something like it—sometime before 1935 A.D."

The correspondence sputtered out.

Pound to Zukofsky: "Call me a liberal and I'll knock yr/constipated block off."

Zukofsky to Pound: "Well, there's no use calling you a liberal—as you say. The next war will show your stand—will show whether you've been a liberal or not."

Pound appears not to have foreseen the war that was coming. There is no reference to its imminence before it began, and none after it started, in *The Letters of Ezra Pound 1907–1941*, although he was to claim later that the purpose of his 1939 visit to the United States was to prevent it.

There are other lacunae. Yeats wrote Lady Dorothy Wellesley on October 8, 1938: "Yesterday morning I had tragic news. Olivia Shakespear has died suddenly. For more than twenty years she has been the center of my life in London." But there is no reference to his wife's mother in Pound's *Letters*. There is no reference to his wife. There is no reference to his daughter. There is no reference to Omar Shakespear Pound, who was twelve when his grandmother died. Neither his father nor his mother came to the funeral; Pound arrived later on family business. Omar had not seen his father since 1930, and was not to see him again until 1945. There is no reference to the death of Yeats in 1939.

four

The Monetary Reformer

———————————— **1** ————————————

*"It is untrue that I, or anybody else in Germany, wanted war in
1939. It was wanted and provoked exclusively by those
international politicians who either came of Jewish
stock, or worked for Jewish interests."*
—From Hitler's political testament, 1945

Pound arrived in New York on the Italian liner *Rex* April 21,
1939. Attired in a double-breasted tweed jacket and powder-blue
trousers, the points of his open shirt draped over his lapels, he
received the press in a lounge chair, head back, legs outstretched.
The question uppermost in everyone's mind was put to him:
would there be war?

"Nothing but devilment can start a war west of the Vistula," he replied. (It will be recalled that the war, which started a few months later, began with the German bombardment of Danzig.) "I'm not making any accusation against anyone. But the bankers and the munitions interests, whoever and wherever they may be, are more responsible for the present talk of war than are the intentions of Mussolini or anyone else." Mussolini, he said, "has a mind with the quickest uptake of any man I know of except Picabia." The reporters looked blank. "Picabia is the man who ties the knots in Picasso's tail."

The usual questions followed about current books and writers.

"I regard the literature of social significance as of no significance. It is pseudo-pink blah. The men who are worth anything today are definitely down on money—writing about money, the problem of money, exchange, gold and silver. I have yet to find a Bolshevik who has written about it."

What did he think of James Joyce?

"When Joyce was writing I ballyhooed him. Not since he retrogressed."

Ernest Hemingway?

"Hemingway is a good guy, but I don't suppose we'd want to meet personally. Spain."

Poets?

"I can name only one poet writing today. I mean E. E. Cummings."

Neither war nor literature was his concern. He had come to the United States to preach Social Credit, and thought that Washington, D.C., was the most effective place to do it in. Thither he went, and as the grandson of a congressman he was courteously received.

His requests for interviews started at the top. President Roosevelt was too busy to see him, but he saw two Senators and enshrined what they said in Canto LXXXIV:

> "an' doan you think he chop an' change all the time
> stubborn az a mule, sah, stubborn as a MULE,
> got th' eastern idea about money"
>   Thus Senator Bankhead
> "am sure I don't know what a man like you
>   would find to *do* here"

said Senator Borah
Thus the solons, in Washington,
on the executive, and on the country, a.d. 1939

He also palavered the Senator from Idaho into his January 29,
1942, broadcast, previously cited: "As my American friend, Senator
Borah, is dead—not that I knew him much save by letter, but I
can still feel his hand on my shoulder just before he was getting
into an elevator in the Senate building, and I can still hear him
saying a couple of days before, saying to me—Borah saying to me—
'Well, I'm sure I don't know what a man like you would find to
do here.' "

He saw Secretary of Agriculture (afterward Vice President)
Henry A. Wallace. Mr. Wallace recalled: "Pound had some ideas
as to proper economic organization but I have forgotten what they
were. He seemed normal enough when he called on me but rather
pessimistic as to the future of the United States."

In an affidavit in support of an application for bail his counsel
stated that Pound "saw such statesmen as Bankhead, Borah,
Bridges, Byrd, Downey, Lodge, MacLeish, Tinkham, Voorhis and
Wallace, all in a vain effort to move the nation's policies toward
paths which he thought were the paths to peace." Pound himself
told the district judge at his first arraignment that he had made the
1939 journey "to keep hell from breaking loose in the world." The
poet Archibald MacLeish was Librarian of Congress in 1939; in
1941, director of the U.S. Office of Facts and Figures, and in 1944,
Assistant Secretary of State.

He attended a session of Congress, but was not impressed. He
went to the Library of Congress and asked to see the librarian in
charge of American history. To him he showed the leaflet containing his "Introductory Text Book" and asked: "Is there a history of
America, whether in one volume or in ten, that contains these four
chapters, or the substance of them?"

The librarian reflected. Then he said, according to Pound, who
related it: "So far as I know, you are the first to have brought together and in relation to each other the four great names of the
greatest Presidents of the Republic."

After Washington, there was a great deal of shuttling back and forth. Mrs. Cummings recalled seeing Pound carrying a pair of rolled-up pajamas in an envelope under his arm. John Slocum, one of the friends he stayed with in New York City, recalled a trip to Englewood, New Jersey, where he and Pound picked up the daughter of an old friend—whose, not specified—then returned and tried to get into the Stork Club. They were refused admission because of Pound's costume. This time, he was not only tieless— he was wearing a shirt with broad purple stripes.

Slocum said: "When I asked him why he had endorsed Il Duce so passionately and so idiotically for the *World Telegram,* he replied: 'They won't pay any attention to me if I don't say something sensational,' which led me to believe that his trip had been underwritten by the Italian Line and/or the Ministry of Propaganda."

2

Pound had left the *Rex* so swiftly after his interview that he did not receive a telegram of welcome John Cournos had sent him, and missed seeing Gorham B. Munson, who arrived at the pier to welcome him in person.

Mr. Munson was the editor of *New Democracy,* the official publication of the American Social Credit Movement, to which Pound was a frequent contributor, and to which his father had directed Zukofsky's steps. Perhaps Munson wished to give Pound a few pointers.

"In three important respects he was a liability," Munson recalled. "Although Social Credit was inherently anti-Fascist and anti-Communist, Pound was trying to combine social credit economic democracy with Fascist political totalitarianism. American Social Creditors did not like that.

"Second, although Pound rated Social Credit as the best economic scheme, he sometimes urged the dated money-stamp scrip scheme of Silvio Gesell as an alternate to Social Credit. Social

Creditors considered the Gesell scheme unsound and authoritarian in nature.

"Third, Pound's anti-Semitism was distasteful. When the American Social Credit Movement was organized in 1936, it officially banned anti-Semites from membership. The same official ban was made by the Social Credit Party of Great Britain headed by John Hargrave."

Mr. Hargrave wrote Munson that Pound's propaganda for Social Credit was "worthless." A spokesman for the British movement wrote recently: "Pound, in my opinion, never was a Social Creditor. He was a 'monetary reformer' who somehow got into the 'credit reform' movement under the impression that the two were the same."

Pound stated in *Money Pamphlet No. 4*, 1942: "I am not going back to Social Credit. The latter was the doorway through which I came to economic curiosity"; and in a broadcast in the same year: "I am not a Social Creditor, I passed by that alley."

He phoned Munson from Ford Madox Ford's apartment on lower Fifth Avenue, and was asked to lunch at the Players Club, on Gramercy Park. He arrived wearing a white sport shirt, no tie, a baggy tweed suit.

"He talked about his stay in Washington where he had been seeing Congressmen in the interest of monetary reform," Munson recalled, "and he talked reassuringly of the international situation. He was not explicit about his Washington interviews, and was chary of names. He did not think war was in the offing."

Pound went to Cambridge, where he stayed with Professor Theodore Spencer, who was also a poet. A student at Harvard, James Laughlin, afterward Pound's publisher, watched them play tennis. "Ted fancied himself a good tennis player," Laughlin recalled, "but Pound beat him." Mrs. Spencer recalled Pound's fascination with her new refrigerator, which included its contents.

Asked whom he would like to meet, Pound said the head of the Economics Department, no professors of English. He was prevailed on by the Department of English to give a reading and by the Department of Speech to make a recording.

Back in New York he played host at Robert's on East Fifty-fifth

Street, where he had previously dined with H. L. Mencken. His party consisted of a silent disciple, Mr. and Mrs. Cummings, and Mr. and Mrs. Max Eastman, whom Pound had asked Cummings to bring. Eastman, who had not met Pound before, found him "attractively curly-headed, almost roly-poly, and with lots of laughter in the corners of his eyes."

All went well until the subject of Fascism came up. Mrs. Eastman—the late Eliena Krylenko, a painter—asked Pound point blank if they hadn't stopped singing in Italy; Cummings thought she had hit upon the tragedy of Pound himself and murmured, "Plus tard, plus tard."

Then Eastman asked: "Don't you, as an alien, escape the regimentation which is the essence of Fascism? I wouldn't say you would greatly enjoy being regimented yourself."

"Fascism only regiments those who can't do anything without it," Pound retorted. "If a man knows how to do anything, it's the essence of Fascism to leave him alone."

He met Zukofsky in the studio of Tibor Serly, the composer. His choice of subject was unfortunate.

Pound had long known about Father Charles E. Coughlin, the "radio priest," whom he admired as a rabble-rouser; now he had the opportunity to hear him. He was, as usual, impressed by anyone with an audience, in this case an immense one—"the score is *reported* of 60,000 telegrams to 800 in favor of Coughlin against the Administration," he had jotted down in Rapallo. He asked Zukofsky if Coughlin could be "educated"—perhaps he meant for Social Credit; Coughlin needed no lessons in Fascism. His publication, *Social Justice,* printed propaganda received from Germany, where he was highly thought of; his talks were based on material supplied by the Nazi newsletter "World Service." Zukofsky retorted: "Whatever you don't know, Ezra, you ought to know *voices.*"

Pound went often to Serly's studio. Mrs. Serly, having watched him consume great quantities of Hungarian pastries, made a "real old-fashioned home-made" strawberry shortcake for him.

"One Saturday night," Serly recalled, "Pound came in a great rush of confusion to my place—he was to go to Hamilton College the next day to receive an honorary degree and had no black shoes, just the big brown shoes he always wore. I finally found a pair to fit him."

3

It was while Pound was in Washington that he received, or at least accepted, the proffer of an honorary degree from his alma mater. He had earlier sent suggestions for the teaching of history and economics, and enclosed his "Introductory Text Book." He stayed at the home of Mr. and Mrs. Edward Root on College Hill. Root, a fellow student in Old French a quarter century before, was now a teacher.

Charles A. Miller, head of the Utica Savings Bank and a Hoover appointee who had been asked to stay on by Roosevelt, was another guest. Pound gave him a lecture on the Douglas Plan, talking so long that Mrs. Root had to interpose, saying, "Charles must have his rest."

Mrs. Root recalled: "Pound came to our house after he had been in Washington where he talked with Senators about credit. He said Representative Tinkham was the only man to be President, and damned the Roosevelts."

On June 9 Pound was interviewed by a reporter from the Utica *Observer-Dispatch*. He talked "quite a little and fiercely about England." He had on a blue blouse and dazzling white shorts. He was having "a very delightful time." Much of it was spent on the college tennis courts.

The commencement exercises were held on June 12 in the Georgian Colonial college chapel. Pound was awarded the honorary degree of Doctor of Letters. The citation was read out:

"Ezra Pound: Native of Idaho, graduate of Hamilton College in the Class of 1905, poet, critic, and prose writer of great distinction. Since completing your college career you have had a life full of significance in the arts. You have found that you could work more happily in Europe than in America and so have lived most of the past thirty years an expatriate making your home in England, France and Italy, but your writings are known wherever English is read.

"Your feet have trodden paths, however, where the great reading public could give you few followers—into Provençal and Italian poetry, into Anglo-Saxon and Chinese. From all these excursions you have brought back treasure. Your translations from the Chinese have, for example, led one of the most gifted of contemporary poets [T. S. Eliot] to call you the inventor of Chinese poetry for our time. Your Alma Mater, however, is an old lady who has not always understood where you have been going, but she has watched you with interest and pride if not always with understanding.

"The larger public has also been at times amazed at your political and economic as well as your artistic credo, and you have retaliated by making yourself—not unintentionally perhaps—their gadfly. Your range of interests is immense, and whether or not your theories of society survive, your name is permanently linked with the development of English poetry in the twentieth century. Your reputation is international, you have guided many poets into new paths, you have pointed new directions, and the historian of the future in tracing the development of your growing mind will inevitably, we are happy to think, be led to Hamilton and to the influence of your college teachers. You have ever been a generous champion of younger writers as well as of artists in other fields, and for this fine and rare human quality and for your own achievements in poetry and prose, we honor you."

President William Harold Cowley placed over Pound's head the buff and blue hood which commemorates the colors of the Revolutionary army.

The traditional alumni luncheon followed. The principal speaker was H. V. Kaltenborn, a veteran news analyst, who had also been honored with a degree. He praised England, whose King and Queen were the guests of the Roosevelts; remarked that "it is written in history that dictatorships shall die but democracies shall live"; and termed the alliance between Germany and Italy of doubtful quality.

Pound interrupted. What did he mean by "doubtful"? Mr. Kaltenborn made an effort to explain, but was further interrupted. Pound had seized the opportunity to praise Mussolini and Fascism. President Cowley had to intervene to stop the angry outbursts of the two honorary doctors.

Pound followed Kaltenborn as speaker.

"You can get the works of Marx and Trotsky in select editions for ten or twenty-five cents," he said. "And yet, while I was abroad, I spent seven years trying to get a copy of John Adams' writings. It is my conviction that you ought to be able to purchase the thoughts and writings of America's founders as easily and cheaply as you can those of subversive propagandists."

He concluded his talk by advocating as required reading in the college curriculum his "Introductory Text Book."

His departure from Clinton was less happy than his arrival. A fellow alumnus offered to drive him to Albany, and on the way invited him to spend a night in his Saratoga home. He recalled afterward: "Our visit was completely senseless and non-productive and I often wonder why I ever got into it." He had been all but overwhelmed by a monologue on economics.

The next morning Pound took the train to New York. The rounds began anew. He was defensive about the incident upstate. Perhaps, as some suggested at the time, he had worn out his welcome. It was a subdued reformer who rode to the pier for the return voyage. John Slocum saw him off.

A request for biographical information had followed Pound from Italy to the United States, and from the United States to Italy; now, from Rapallo, after a stopover in Siena, he replied to the publishers of *Twentieth Century Authors*. He did not enlighten them.

"When a writer merits mention in a work of reference," he wrote in rage, "his work IS his autobiography, it is his first person record. If you can't print my one page 'Introductory Text Book' enclosed (and to appear here) then your profession of wanting an authentic record is mere bunk, and fit only to stand with the infamies that have raged in America since [Andrew] Johnson was kicked out of the White House, and in especial throughout the degration [sic] of the American state and system by Wilson and Roosevelt."

He also attacked "the great and dastardly betrayal of the American people and the American system, by the trick clause, and the Bank Act of February 25, 1863."

The subject reappeared in his broadcast of May 15, 1943: "We have heard of wars for commodities and wars for gold. We have heard much less of a secret war that the United States lost in 1863, while the boys in blue and the boys in gray were obligingly dying and taking the spotlight [in a] civil war [that] was, at that time, a world record for carnage and both sides well vanquished. The control of the national credit, control of the national currency, the national purchasing power, passed right away from the people and right out of the control of the national and responsible government."

He was right, though tardy. By the National Banking Acts of 1863 and 1864, Congress, say the historians Allan Nevins and Henry Steele Commager, "swept away the independent banking system dear to Jacksonian democrats and substituted one more favorable to private bankers. To give a clear field to the notes of the national banks, state-bank notes were taxed out of existence."

As for the trick clause: greenbacks, although selling for as little as forty cents on the dollar, were still legal tender for the purchase of government bonds. The bonds, both principal and interest, were redeemable in gold. Fortunes were made by those "in the know."

The editors of *Twentieth Century Authors* did as they were told, even to placing the "Introductory Text Book" where Pound had designated it on the page—"to appear here." An account of his life and work being still needed, the editors wrote it themselves.

War or no war, the letters poured forth from Rapallo. Ever present was the fixed idea, sometimes in grotesque garb. He wrote Richard Aldington that the Germans were about to sack London and hang Churchill "on the gold exchange." H. G. Wells had also been his friend. After glancing at *The Work, Wealth, and Happiness of Mankind* (eight years after its publication) he wrote its author:

"Waaal, you are pretty messy. . . . Naturally you are weak on Doug and Gesell because English do *not* read books by men younger than themselves. . . . But for affection's sake, I *will* read the damn thing carefully if you wd. like a careful criticism of some of the sloppy paragraphs."

The affection was soon forgotten, as we have seen; Wells was transformed into "Chubby" Wells, one of the "liberal stooges."

five

The Propagandist

1

"The time has come to put a formal end to the countenancing of Ezra Pound. For a number of years, at the beginning of the magazine, he was associated with Poetry, *and the association was valuable on both sides. Then he quarreled with us, as he has quarreled with everyone, yet continued to use the magazine as an outlet for the publication of his* Cantos *and other poems. Now, so far as we and the rest of the English-speaking world of letters are concerned, he has effectively written* finis *to his long career as inspired* enfant terrible.*"*
—From the editorial in the April, 1942, issue

The broadcasts of record—those monitored by the Federal Communications Commission from December 7, 1941, to July 25, 1943, when the Department of Justice moved to indict Pound—total 125.

Many are repetitious, rambling, or fatuous; but in some of them he was almost prescient about postwar developments. Several are in the nature of "replies" to the speeches of American officials, as though he alone had the answers to problems which the United States, at war, found so anxious and so formidable.

There was still another kind of broadcast that he made. Pound did not always have the material for a talk; talk he must, and he substituted literary essays already published or scheduled for publication, and at least one Canto—XLV, which is about usury.

It is possible to make a selection dealing with writers, with literature, and with culture generally; this has been done, in a pamphlet printed in Italy by a friend. It is also possible to marshal more or less convincing evidence that Pound on the air was merely voicing personal views on American politics, politicians, and economics—"international money power," as he termed it; this, too, has been done, by a friend in the United States. The Department of Justice, however, made an entirely different kind of selection, and was to charge that Pound "knowingly, intentionally, wilfully, unlawfully, feloniously, traitorously and treasonably did adhere to the enemies of the United States."

February 3, 1942

"You are at war for the duration of the Germans' pleasure. You are at war for the duration of Japan's pleasure. Nothing in the western world, nothing in the whole of our Occident, can help you to dodge that. Nothing can help you dodge it."

April 16, 1942

"For the United States to be making war on Italy and on Europe is just plain nonsense, and every native-born American of American stock knows that it is plain downright damn nonsense. And for this state of things Franklin Roosevelt is more than any other one man responsible."

April 23, 1942

"The drift of Mr. Archibald MacLeish's remarks towards the end of March seems fairly clear. He has been given a gangster's brief and he has been entrusted with the defense of a gang of criminals and he is a-doing his damnedest. I object and have objected to the crime, regardless of who may be related to the men who have committed it, and I accept the conditions of the debate—namely, that the Morgenthau-Lehman gang control 99 per cent of all means of communication inside the United States and that they can drown out and buy out nearly all opposition; on top of which Roosevelt has, characteristically, resorted to blackmail. Any man who does not accept the gigantic frauds perpetrated by the Morgenthau-Roosevelt treasury is to be held up as a traitor to the United States.

"The reply is that any man who submits to Roosevelt's treason to the public commits a breach of citizen's duty. There is no connection between submittin' to the Roosevelt-Morgenthau frauds and patriotism. There is no connection between such submission and winning this war—or any other. There is no patriotism in submittin' to the prolonged and multiple frauds of the Roosevelt administration and to try to make the present support of these frauds figure as loyalty to the American Union, to the American Constitution, to the American heritage, is just so much dirt or bunkum. Doubtless the tactics of evasion will be used to the uttermost—but if the American people submit to either or both of these wheezes the American people will be mugs.

"There are several historic facts which the opulent of the Morgenthau-Lehman gang would do well to dig up. Our Mr. Mac-Leish has not gone out—all out—for the printing of the defects of American history in handy and available volumes, so there are several historic facts which the opulent of the Morgenthau swindle would be well advised to extract and use.

"Of course, for you to go looking for my point—points—of my bi-weekly talk in the maze of Jew-governed American radio transmissions is like looking for one needle in a whole flock of haystacks. And your press is not very open. However, if some lone watcher or listener on Back Bay or on top of the Blue Ridge does hear me, I suggest he make notes and ask Advocate Archibald whether it does win anything to have the people pay two dollars for every dollar spent by the government. I ask whether the spirit of '76 is helped by a-floodin' the lower ranks of the Navy with bridge-sweepin's;

whether war is won by mercantilist ethics and, in any case, whether men like Knox and Stimson and Morgenthau can be expected to fill the heart of youth with martial ardor and spirit of sacrifice.

"I ask Archie to say openly why he handed out four billion dollars in excess profits on the gold [word or words missing] between 1932 and 1940, handing it to a dirty gang of kikes and hyper-kikes on the London gold exchange firms. Why is that expected to help Americanism? Or why should it be regarded as a model of devotion to the American spirit? Or why should any honest American vote for the continuance of that swindle or of keeping in office the men and kikes who were responsible for putting it over the people?

"And that, of course, is not the whole story of Roosevelt, Lehman, Baruch, Morgenthau, dipping into the country's resources. The break with our tradition exemplified by Donovan's intrigues in Yugoslavia is no Cornelia's jewel. In fact, all Roosevelt's talk about patriotism is nothing but the gilding on the outside of base metal. Keeping Roosevelt in the White House is not essential to winning the war. The two things can be considered quite apart one from the other.

"Had you had the sense to eliminate Roosevelt and his Jews or the Jews and their Roosevelt at the last election, you would not now be at war. That is one point. But to suppose that you will win the war by goin' on bein' mugs in any and every internal conflict, to suppose that you will strengthen the United States abroad by submittin' to continued internal bleedin' and swindlin' is just so much hokum or nonsense.

"The first step towards a bright new world, so far as the rising American generation is concerned, is to git on to Roosevelt and all his works, and the second is to eliminate him and all his damned gang from public life in America. The alternative is annihilation for the youth of America and the end of everything decent the U.S. ever stood for. If you allow yourself to be dazzled, if you are persuaded to identify the Morgenthau-Baruch control of the U.S. by secret committees for the war birds with victory, then you are mugs. If you confuse these things and the promise of Army contracts even with national defense, then you are plain downright suckers.

"I shall be highly interested to see whether Archibald takes up any of the points of this discourse. If he don't, some bright lad ought to help him. Someone ought to dig up a point here and there."

May 5, 1942

"The kike, and the unmitigated evil that has been centered in London since the British government set on the Red Indians to murder the American frontier settlers, has herded the Slavs, the Mongols, the Tartar openly against Germany and Poland and Finland. And secretly against all that is decent in America, against the total American heritage. This is my war all right. I've been in it for twenty years—my granddad was in it before me."

May 10, 1942

"The next peace will not be based on international lending. Get that for one. The next peace will not be based on international lending, and England certainly will have nothing whatever to say about what its terms are. Neither, I think, will simple-hearted Joe Stalin, not wholly trusted by the kikery which is his master."

May 26, 1942

"Every hour that you go on with this war is an hour lost to you and your children. And every sane act you commit is committed in homage to Mussolini and Hitler. Every reform, every lurch toward the just price, toward the control of a market, is an act of homage to Mussolini and Hitler. They are your leaders, however much you think you are conducted by Roosevelt or told up by Churchill. You follow Mussolini and Hitler in every constructive act of your government."

May 31, 1942

"The melting pot in America may have been a noble experiment, though I very much doubt it. At any rate it is lost."

June 28, 1942

"You are not going to win this war. None of our best minds ever thought you could win it. You have never had a chance in this war."

July 2, 1942

"I am not arguing, I am just telling you, one of these days you will have to start thinking about the problem of race, breed, preservation."

July 6, 1942

"There is so much that the United States does not know. This war is [the] fruit of such vast incomprehension, such tangled ignorance, so many strains of undoing, I'm held up in rage by the delaying needed to change a typing ribbon, so much is there that ought to be put into young America's head. I don't know what to put down. I can't write two scripts at once. Necessary dates are always coming in pell-mell. I try to get too much into ten minutes. I can turn vague and look at a summary. Maybe if I had more sense of form, legal training, God knows what, I could get the matter across the Atlantic or the bally old Channel."

July 14, 1942

"You are in black darkness and confusion, you have been hugger-muggered and scarum-shouted into a war, and you know nothing about it. You know nothing about the forces that caused it. Or you know next to nothing. I am in the agonized position of an observer who has worked twenty-five years to prevent it, but I'm not the only observer who has so striven. Apparently no man could prevent it, that is, up to the point that it was not prevented. But a belief in destiny does not necessarily imply a belief that we have no duty; that we should not attempt to learn; that we should sit supine before an age-old evil. Given a little more knowledge, given the elimination of a small number of shysters, the war need not have happened. . . . Now what are you fighting for? Fighting for the congressional system? Fighting for parliamentary system? I doubt it. Democracy? Now what do you mean by democracy? Men might fight for justice. Many men fight from greed; not their own greed. Fight from instinct. Well, that's O.K. up to a point. Fight for survival. That's health. Men ought to fight for survival. And for racial survival. But are you fighting for racial survival? I doubt it. I doubt if you've got to thinking about racial survival. Well, I could help you start thinking."

July 20, 1942

"You ought not to be at war against Italy. You ought not to be giving or ever to have given the slightest or most picayune aid to any man or nation engaged in waging war against Italy. You are doing it for the sake of a false accountancy system."

July 22, 1942

"Europe calling. . . . Ezra Pound speaking.

"I hear that my views are shared, most of them, by a large number of my compatriots, so it would seem, or maybe an increasing number of my compatriots. And there is a comforting thought on a warm day in a fine climate. I should hate to think that all America has gone haywire. I should like to feel that the American race in North America, in the North American continent, had some wish towards survival. That they wanted there to be a United States of tomorrow. . . .

"Well, you have been fed on lies, for twenty years you have been fed on lies, and I don't say maybe. And Mr. Squirmy and Mr. Slime are still feeding it to you right over the B.B.C. radio, and every one of the Jew radios of Schenectady, New York and Boston —and Boston was once an American city; that was when it was about the size of Rapallo. . . .

"And how much liberty have you got, anyhow? And as to the arsenal—are you the arsenal of democracy or of judeocracy? And who rules your rulers? Where does public responsibility end, and what races can mix in America without ruin of the American stock, the American brain? Who is organized? What say have you in the choice of your rulers? What control of their policy? And who does own most of your press and your radio? E. P. asking you."

March 19, 1943

"Alice James, the great Henry's sister, complained that we Americans wouldn't show moral indignation. That is, the time when she would get all set to have an American show moral in-

dignation, the American would just fold up [and] act dead. . . .
I take it I sometimes do display some sort of indignation. . . .
And when a man comes out and says no American boy shall be
sent to fight outside the country and a few months or years later
you hear him [word garbled] Marines and American soldiers in all
parts of the globe, ain't it wonderful.

"Am I expected to display moral indignation? Here [word or
words missing] again three hundred corpses floating about in the
sea off the harbor of [blank in transcript]; well, are these only two
hundred? Why, in a year or so there'll be thousands and thousands
of corpses floating all over the ocean. Ain't it wonderful?

"Ain't it wonderful? Aw, what are you waiting for? Waiting for
him to receive Maisky and Litvinov and other high diplomats with
feathers in his hair? What'ya waiting for? Ezra Pound speaking."

March 26, 1943

"Quite apart from military operations, apart from the result of
military operations, from the possible results of any military operations that may occur—the American people appear to have
suffered crushing defeat at the hands of the financiers."

March 30, 1943

"What the British and the Americans are doing on the Tunisian
front reminds us very much of the big fellow who, drunk and be-
fuddled, tries to get after his smaller adversary, and instead falls
into a ditch and remains there, not quite understanding what has
happened to him. The British forces have occupied the Mareth
Line; the British forces are running after Marshal Rommel's
troops; the British forces are surrounding the Afrika Korps; and
so on and so forth. But when one comes down to brass tacks, one
finds that what has really happened is quite a different story. Marshal Rommel, who is nobody's fool when it comes to fighting any
kind of a battle, has considered it would be better to take up new
positions, which will make the plans of General Montgomery fail.
We must admit that it would have been very nice if Marshal Rommel had remained on the Mareth Line, and had been caught in the
rear. For the Allies, this would have been too nice for words. But

it didn't happen. And now something else has to be cogitated to finish the fight in Tunisia, and give the British and American public something to shout about. The one point which is of interest, and which should be in the mind of every Britisher and American, is the fact that the losses suffered by the Allies in these battles are terrific."

On May 4, 1943, while American, British, and French troops were driving toward Tunis and Bizerte, Pound asked: "What are you doing in the war at all? What are you doing in Africa? Who amongst you has the nerve or the sense to do something that would conduce to getting you out of it before you are mortgaged up to the neck and over it? Every day of war is a dead day as well as a death day. More death, more future servitude, less and less of American liberty of any variety."

May 8, 1943

"There is not an ounce or atom of honesty in either Churchill or Roosevelt. Most of the reasons for England and America being in the war are unconfessable and indecent. . . . A clean England and a clean United States might collaborate in a new world, but it will take a hell of a lot of Sapolio to wash off the mess made by Roosevelt and Churchill. I'm telling you, I'm not giving you the Axis point of view."

–––––––––––––––––––– **2** ––––––––––––––––––––

Pound's talks had become a way of life—social as well as political. He participated in programs which were not his own, and in which he was merely a supernumerary, a hanger-on, a butt.

Undersecretary of State Sumner Welles had made an important speech. Even before he had the text of it Pound was eager to "reply." He brought the subject up without knowing Welles's subject. He did not know where Welles had spoken. He did not even know he—Pound—was on the air.

The following short-wave radio broadcast was beamed to England, May 12, 1943, 7:20 EWT, and monitored here:

ANNOUNCER. Around the microphone with me tonight are Al Sanders, whom you already know, and Ezra Pound, who spoke to you last time, on this same broadcast.

POUND. I spoke to you, I thought. I was not talking to anybody but the boys around the microphone.

ANNOUNCER. Well, exactly; but you know perfectly well—at least we hope—that there might be a few people who want to get a little bit of learning into their heads, by benefiting from his wisdom [aside to Sanders?].

POUND. Shall we say something overheard, what?

ANNOUNCER. Something overheard—exactly. What did we speak about last time, Al?

SANDERS. Before we get into any particular subject, I have a question to ask Mr. Pound. I heard you last night on a broadcast to America.

POUND. Do you mean to say anybody here listens to my broadcasts to America?

SANDERS. I do. Of course. I—maybe I'm a special case. But I do.

POUND. I always thought you were a special case. But—even so.

SANDERS. Kidding aside, I want to know one thing. You kept on talking about a speech made by the Undersecretary of State of the United States.

POUND. Well, I mean he's called the Undersecretary, but I mean I don't imagine Mr. Hull has much to do with running that department.

SANDERS. I think Mr. Hull is a nice old guy. I remember reading a whole story of his life in Life.

POUND. His life—I mean to say—

SANDERS. Yes, he's a Tennessee boy and they give him quite a write-up.

POUND. No doubt they'd give him quite a write-up, but what does he do in the State Department?

SANDERS. He gives it tone.

POUND. He gives it tone?

(Laughter.)

ANNOUNCER. What kind of tone, Al?

SANDERS. First, I want to get through my question. Then we'll discuss Mr. Hull. (*To Pound*) I want to know why you call Mr. Sumner Welles Mr. Sumner Wel-les. Don't you know about it? Have you been here in Italy so long you don't even know how to pronounce your own countryman's name?

POUND. I suppose that if he puts that extra "e" in, he put it there for effect—I suppose he wanted people to pronounce it that way.

SANDERS. What do you mean, he put it in?

POUND. I didn't think he was born with an "e" in his name. I thought that "e" came out of a name of some Cabinet minister of early American historical times.

SANDERS. Sumner went "society" on us?

POUND. I don't know anything about "society." I mean, I've been out of that country for a long time. I thought it was—might say— historic, what do you call it, a bit of old-lace-and-lavender-Colonial touch, I suppose you might say. Qualifying for the Daughters of the American Revolution or something.

SANDERS. Now tell us, Mr. Pound, you really think that when Mr. Welles made his speech—where was it exactly, at Toledo, wasn't it?

POUND. I got mixed up. I kept calling it Toronto, but I think it was Toledo or—

SANDERS. What do you think, when he made that speech? Did he really take it that Europe, or rather the Axis countries, would take it seriously?

POUND. God knows, a man makes a speech in Ohio, in Toledo, Ohio, where the presidents come from—.

SANDERS. Is that a hint for a future candidate, in case FDR gets sidetracked?

POUND. Well, I suppose Mr. Wel-les or Welles, if you want to call him that, looks for a continuation of his job and hopes for a Democratic victory some time or other.

SANDERS. But you think that he would hope for a continuation of his job with FDR in the seat?

POUND. I reckon those Democrats would like to keep the seat, though they don't care much who runs it, but as long as they've got a permanency, they'd keep it.

SANDERS. As long as we brought the subject up, what do you mean [by Democrats]? A couple of years ago there were a lot of Democrats who wouldn't recognize FDR as a Democrat, if he saw them.

POUND. Well, I mean the New Deal, er . . .

SANDERS. A description of *what* kind of a New Deal we can't put over the radio.

POUND. Some of the things in the New Deal were all right—I mean, even Mr. Hamilton Fish said the New Deal for—I think he said—it was all right for nearly two years. At any rate—

SANDERS. I dare say.

POUND. I'd call it socialist then, er, Mr. Roosevelt's prime aim in life. Which do you mean? Are you talking about the hard-shelled Carter Glass, who wanted to get back to gold because the Republicans dote on him?

SANDERS. I mean the average southern Democrat. I've talked with a good many Democrats who never believed that Mr. Roosevelt was much of a Democrat.

POUND. Not a Democrat in the dictionary sense of the word. He's not a man who cares anything about the welfare of his people, I don't think.

SANDERS. Well, his whole program was got up on a basis—

POUND. Yes, I know, he had a program, but maybe John Caldwell Calhoun was the last Democrat.

SANDERS. You said a very just thing, I think, Mr. Pound, when you said that he didn't really have the welfare of the people at heart. I think that is one of the main things one can find fault with FDR about. I think that a lot of people consider that FDR might have done very much better by his people if he hadn't pushed them into the war.

POUND. I didn't want him to get into the war. God knows, this

war was not made for my comfort or for anybody else's that I can
see.

SANDERS. Well now, the English, or rather the British—I wonder how they feel about it? There seems to be a slight discrepancy
of ideas between the British and Americans at this moment.

POUND. If the British can't get a good lunch at the Savoy, why, I
reckon they'd go round to the Berkeley.

SANDERS. Yes, that's right.

POUND. That is—well, I mean the English can go to the Savoy,
where there are only English.

SANDERS. How many are there, what's the percentage of them,
er?

POUND. It isn't a question of percentage—the English is, after
all, a constitutional monarchy. The people in England haven't
got anything to say about running it.

SANDERS. No, that's quite true, the way they haven't got anything
to say about running it in the United States, either.

POUND. Haven't we? Remember those—no, you're too young.
But when they were running—the "Yellow" crew—in the New
York *Journal,* back in 1890—they used to run a funny kind of
poem, in two lines, a little rhyme:

> In the days of Charlemagne
> Did the people drink champagne?

Guess again.

SANDERS. That rhyme can be applied every day.

POUND. In the days of old champagne, did the people get away?
Nay, nay.

ANNOUNCER. Don't you think that, as Al says, that applies to
people at the present time?

POUND. Not if the directors of Kuhn, Loeb & Co . . . Who are
out in the front line trenches, getting decimated?

SANDERS. Well, the founders of Kuhn, Loeb—.

POUND. The kernel of the whole business.

SANDERS. Kuhn, Loeb brings up to your mind, my mind, to
every man with imagination, international finance. Now, we're

all agreed that the international bankers, either part of one big family, or of one big sect or race or lodge, or whatever you want to call it—.

POUND. There are family ties between some of them.

SANDERS. Are all tied together in the United Nations. We are all agreed on that—I'm sure we agree so today and for the future. If that is so, as we say, how come that there's so much discrepancy of outside views among the different United Nations, among the people of the United Nations?

POUND. But the people get it in the neck all around. When they won't pay up 60 per cent interest, under the impression they're paying 6, then they get pressed into war, or they have Russia stirred up to blackmail the people who won't toe the line.

SANDERS. Don't you think the whole set-up is also very convenient preparatory measure for any future wars? The United Nations, on the surface, are fighting together, and on the under surface, as everyone sees, they are fighting against each other. The British are accusing the Americans of trying to grab the British Empire, and the Americans feel that they are being taken for a ride by the British.

ANNOUNCER. What about the Russians—what do they feel?

POUND. I don't understand the Slavic temperament, but the people who know least are the ones who get into the war quickest.

SANDERS. You know it's a fact, Mr. Pound, that there—the center of world finance used to be in the City of London?

POUND. There was a lot of finance in Paris that wasn't exactly separate. London became very dominant.

SANDERS. Don't you think that, now, has shifted slightly?

POUND. I thought it was generally agreed that the shift was scheduled and that—

SANDERS. You think it was scheduled?

POUND. I think a lot of Jews have now got their money in [transcriber's guess: Argentina].

SANDERS. Yes, I think that's probably true.

ANNOUNCER. How do you link up the so-called United Nations? From the financial point of view, how do you get Russia into the picture?

POUND. They want Russia to kill off the Germans.

SANDERS. In other words—[Germans] to kill off the Russians?

POUND. Secondary, they don't mind Russia being weakened. But Russia is the hammer held over the head of these rebellious Germans and rebellious Europeans.

SANDERS. And rebellious Italians.

POUND. Yes—rebellious Italians, yes.

SANDERS. In other words, you think that there's a British-Russo *mariage de convenance*.

POUND. I don't know that I'd go as far as to call it a marriage—call it a liaison, if you like.

SANDERS. They go to bed together.

ANNOUNCER. Well, if you like to call it that, but they certainly don't see things eye to eye in many other things.

SANDERS. Oh no, the next war is very nicely secured—this er, er, Hank Wallace began to see signs of trouble on the horizon.

ANNOUNCER. Don't you think that any one war is made by just [words missing]. Wars are part of a process, take long preparation.

POUND. Not so long [words missing] to work a curve of acceleration.

SANDERS. In other words, we're fighting a war to start more wars.

POUND. Undoubtedly Italy was trying to stop that process. New York and London are undoubtedly fighting a war to maintain the process of having wars once in so often, whenever it suits international finance.

ANNOUNCER. Yes, I think that's very clear, Mr. Pound. I'm afraid that our time is up. I want to thank Mr. Pound for what he said, and Mr. Sanders. And good-night everybody.

Transcriptions of Pound's broadcasts, Dec. 7, 1941–July 25, 1943, are available on a Library of Congress microfilm. Memovox recordings are in the National Archives.

six

United States *vs.*
Ezra Pound

———— 1 ————

Pound was indicted for treason twice, the first time on July 26, 1943:

The Grand Jurors for the United States of America duly impaneled and sworn in the District Court of the United States for the District of Columbia and inquiring for that District upon their oath present;

That Ezra Pound, the defendant herein, at Rome, Italy, and other places within the territory of the Kingdom of Italy, and, as hereinafter described, in the District of Columbia, within the jurisdiction of this Court, and at other places throughout the United States and elsewhere, continuously, and at all times during the period beginning on the 11th day of December, 1941, and continuing thereafter to and including the date of the presentment and filing of this indictment, under the circumstances and conditions and in the manner and by the means hereinafter set forth, then and there being a citizen of the United States, and a person owing allegiance to the United States, in violation of his said duty of allegiance, knowingly, intentionally, wilfully, unlawfully, feloniously, traitorously, and treasonably did adhere to the enemies of the United States, to wit, the Kingdom of Italy, its counsellors, armies, navies, secret agents, representatives, and subjects, and the military allies of the said Kingdom of Italy, including the Government of the German Reich and the Imperial Government of Japan, with which the United States at all times since December 11, 1941, have been at war, giving to the said enemies of the United States aid and comfort within the United States and elsewhere.

The burden of the specifications which followed, and the statement with which each specification ends, was:

The said defendant asserted, among other things, in substance, that citizens of the United States should not support the United States in the conduct of the said war.

Seven other American citizens were indicted with him, two of them women, all for broadcasting from Germany. Five of them, like Pound, were born in the United States. Attorney General Francis Biddle told the press:

"It should be clearly understood that these indictments are based not only on the content of the propaganda statements—the lies and falsifications which were uttered—but also on the simple fact that these people have freely elected, at a time when their country is at war, to devote their services to the cause of the enemies of the United States. They have betrayed the first and most sacred obligation of American citizenship."

Like many Italians, but without running the risk of imprisonment they did, Pound listened to the BBC to get uncensored news, and it was from a BBC broadcast that he learned of his indictment. He did not know his talks had been monitored. He wrote Mr. Biddle on August 4 (the letter was left by him at the Swiss legation in Rome, which forwarded it to the Secretary of State):

I understand that I am under indictment for treason. I have done my best to get an authentic report of your statement to this effect. And I wish to place the following facts before you.

I do not believe that the simple fact of speaking over the radio, wherever placed, can in itself constitute treason. I think that must depend on what is said, and on the motives for speaking.

I obtained the concession to speak over Rome radio with the following proviso. Namely that nothing should be asked of me contrary to my conscience or contrary to my duties as an American citizen. I obtained a declaration on their part of a belief in "the free expression of opinion by those qualified to have an opinion."

The legal mind of the Attorney General will understand the interest inherent in this distinction, as from unqualified right of expression.

This declaration was made several times in the announcement of my speeches; with the declaration "He will not be asked to say anything contrary to his conscience, or contrary to his duties as an American citizen" (Citizen of the U.S.).

These conditions have been adhered to. The only time I had an opinion as to what might be interesting as subject matter, I was asked whether I would speak of religion. This seemed to me hardly my subject, though I did transmit on one occasion some passages from Confucius, under the title "The Organum of Confucius."

I have not spoken with regard to *this* war, but in protest against a system which creates one war after another, in series and in system. I have not spoken to the troops, and have not suggested that the troops should mutiny or revolt.

The whole basis of democratic or majority government assumes that the citizen shall be informed of the facts. I have not claimed to know all the facts, but I have claimed to know some of the facts which are an essential part of the total that should be known to the people.

I have for years believed that the American people should be better informed as to Europe, and informed by men who are not tied to a special interest or under definite control.

The freedom of the press has become a farce, as everyone knows that the press is controlled, if not by its titular owners, at least by the advertisers.

Free speech under modern conditions becomes a mockery if it does not include the right of free speech over the radio.

And this point is worth establishing. The assumption of the right to punish and take vengeance regardless of the area of jurisdiction is dangerous. I do not mean in a small way; but for the nation.

I returned to America before the war to protest against particular forces then engaged in trying to create war and to make sure that the U.S.A. should be dragged into it.

Arthur Kitson's[1] testimony before the Cunliffe and MacMillan commissions[2] was insufficiently known. Brooks Adams[3] brought to light several currents in history that should be better known. The course of events following the foundation of the Bank of England should be known, and considered in sequence: the suppression of colonial paper money, especially in Pennsylvania! [4] The similar curves following the Napoleonic wars, and our Civil War and Versailles need more attention.

We have not the right to drift into another error similar to that of the Versailles Treaty.

We have, I think, the right to a moderate expansion including defence of the Caribbean, the elimination of foreign powers from the American continent, but such expansion should not take place at the cost of deteriorating or ruining the internal structure of the U.S.A. The ruin of markets, the perversions of trade routes, in fact all the matters on which my talks have been based is of importance to the American citizen; whom neither you nor I should betray either in time of war *or* peace. I may say in passing that I took out a life membership in the American Academy of Social and Political Science in the hope of obtaining fuller discussion of some of these issues, but did not find them ready for full and frank expression of certain vital elements in the case; this may in part have been due to their incomprehension of the nature of the case.

At any rate a man's duties increase with his knowledge. A war between the U.S. and Italy is monstrous and should not have occurred. And a peace without justice is no peace but merely a prelude to future wars. Someone must take count of these things. And having taken count must act on his knowledge; admitting that his knowledge is partial and his judgment subject to error.

---

1 British writer on Social Credit.

2 Read, MacMillan Committee (1929).

3 Henry Brooks Adams, American historian.

4 Biddle was a Philadelphian.

2

It was too late for explanations. A wide net had been cast for him, and it was only a matter of time before he would be apprehended by *partigiani* or American troops. A cable dated September 17 informed the Commanding General of the North African Theater of Operations, General Jacob L. Devers, of Pound's indictment, and General Devers informed the Commanding General of the United States Fifth Army.

The initiative for all eight indictments appears to have come from the War Department—with good reason, since the broadcasts from Germany and Italy were also beamed to American troops at home and abroad; Pound's comments, in particular, about the landings in North Africa were heard by soldiers and sailors who took part in that action, with uneasiness and indignation.

By January of 1943, Major General J. A. Ulio, the Adjutant General, had circulated a confidential report, based on G–2 memoranda, "to provide information which will be valuable for punitive action" and "to inform our responsible officials of the activities and personal histories of these traitors." Inquiries followed from a number of government agencies. To Lawrence M. C. Smith, Chief, Special War Policies Unit, War Division, Federal Bureau of Investigation, General Ulio wrote, February 2, 1943:

The report was classified as "confidential" to prevent premature and fragmentary publicity. The opinion of the War Department is that, unless definite action is taken such as indictments showing a determination to punish these individuals, public discussion of them, as frequently occurs, gives them the advertising which they crave and increases their listener audience in this and other countries.

The War Department is in entire accord with any action which the Department of Justice may take to punish these individuals. The War Department hopes that the report will be of value in such proceedings and is of the opinion that such parts of it as the Department of Justice decides will add to the general contempt for these individuals should be made public when the indictments are announced.

The Secretary of War replied on January 26, 1943, to a letter from the Attorney General making certain inquiries regarding this same report.

On January 24, 1944, Attorney General Biddle asked the Secretary of War for prompt notification should Pound be taken into custody by the military. On February 9 the request was forwarded to General Devers, together with a brief personal history, description and F.B.I. photograph of Pound. The Adjutant General wrote:

It will be noted that the Attorney General wishes certain action taken in the event that Pound should be taken into custody, and that upon the receipt by the Department of Justice of the requested information, further consideration will be given to the advisability of effecting Pound's return to the United States.

General Devers replied, February 25:

Reference your letter of 9 February 1944 concerning activities of Dr. Ezra Pound and desire of Attorney General for certain information in the event of his capture, you are advised that the Commanding General of the United States Fifth Army has again been informed by cable that he is wanted on an indictment charging him with treason and in the event of his capture to notify the Theater Commander immediately.

The F.B.I. photograph of Dr. Pound is being reproduced. It will be distributed with other descriptive data through the Provost Marshal and G–2 sections.

The "descriptive data" included: height, five feet ten and one-half inches; forehead, broad; eyes, grey-green; nose, straight; mouth, mustached; chin, bearded; complexion, fair; face, oval.

The invasion of North Africa was followed by the invasion of Italy. The Germans descended from the north. When they reached Rapallo, Pound was "chased out" (his own words) and with his wife went to Sant' Ambrogio, in the nearby hills, where they lived until the spring of 1945. It was in Sant' Ambrogio that the *partigiani* came for him.

3

Pound has given different accounts of the way in which he was taken into custody by the Americans. One is that he escaped from the *partigiani,* which may have been lucky for him; another is that he surrendered to an American soldier advancing with the partisans. He was taken to a command post at Lavagna, and from there to the Counter Intelligence Center at Genoa, where he was interviewed by an F.B.I. agent.

The first item in the May 17th G–2 Journal, Headquarters 92nd Infantry Division, listing "Incidents, msgs, Orders, etc.," reads: "Ezra Pound in custody of CIC, 92nd Div since 3 May 45. Signed statement and pertinent documents obtained. Request disposition."

The second item reads: "Near our CP Campomorone there is a partisan headquarters. We have information which leads us to believe they are holding quick court and executing people. Investigation of the above by Lt Smith and Capt Gordon (British) lead to no confirmation. The partisan military command of Campomorone admits making political arrests but insists that they are not holding courts. They do interrogate to see whether they should be confined to the jail in Genoa or released. They say they have conducted no executions. Capt Gordon warned them of spoiling the good name of the partisans. This was personally conveyed to Lt Col Ray who is inclined to disbelieve the partisan statement."

What Pound told the agent at their interview remains locked in the files of the Federal Bureau of Investigation in Washington. He probably spoke freely; he spoke freely to a reporter who was permitted to see him on the sixth floor of an office building overlooking the main square of Genoa:

"There is no doubt which I preferred between Mussolini and Roosevelt. In my radio broadcasts I spoke in favor of the economic construction of Fascism. Mussolini was a very human, imperfect character who lost his head.

"Winston believes in the maximum of injustice enforced with the maximum of brutality.

"Hitler was a martyr. Like many martyrs, he held extreme views."

This was on May 8; Pound had been in custody five days. Disposition of his case was requested May 17, as we have seen; five months later he was almost released for lack of instructions. The following glossary will be useful in connection with the dispatches received and sent by the Allied Force Headquarters and Mediterranean Theater of Operations message centers, Caserta, Italy:

G–1: Administration
G–2: Military Intelligence
G–5: Military Government
CIC: Counter Intelligence Center
CP: Command Post
AFHQ: Allied Force Headquarters
CG MTOUSA: Commanding General, Mediterranean Theater of Operations
AGWAR: Adjutant General, War Department

ALEXANDER: Field Marshal Earl Alexander, Allied Commander
PMG: Provost Marshal General

May 19, 1945
FROM: 15 ARMY GROUP
TO: AFHQ, INFO G–5
    For G–2
Doctor EZRA POUND captured 3 May by partisans is now in custody of CIC 92 Division. [Name of F.B.I. agent, deleted] has obtained signed statement and pertinent documents and is awaiting decision from WASHINGTON regarding disposal.

May 21, 1945
FROM: FIFTH ARMY
TO: CG MTOUSA

Awaiting orders for disposition from your Headquarters for DR. EZRA POUND, War Criminal, held by 92 Division.

May 21, 1945
TO FOR ACTION: AGWAR WASHINGTON
SIGNED: ALEXANDER

In custody Provost Marshal here is EZRA POUND.

Reference AGWAR cable of 14th May.

Investigation completed. Statement by POUND and documentary evidence airmailed FORNEY 21st May. Request information POUND's further disposition soonest.

The reply came in the form of instructions which, in the light of subsequent events, appear to have been ill advised. They were to prove fatal to the government's case.

May 22, 1945
TO FOR ACTION: CG FIFTH ARMY
                    CG REPLACEMENT AND TRAINING COMMAND
SIGNED: CG MTOUSA

American Civilian Doctor EZRA LOOMIS POUND reference Fifth Army cable 2006 under federal grand jury indictment for treason.

Transfer without delay under guard to MTOUSA Disciplinary Training Center for confinement pending disposition instructions. Exercise utmost security measures to prevent escape or suicide. No press interviews authorized. Accord no preferential treatment.

May 27, 1945
FROM: FIFTH ARMY
TO: CG MTOUSA

Doctor EZRA POUND delivered to MTOUSA DTC 1500 hours 24 May this year.

He was now out of the Military Government and Intelligence branches of the Army, and in the hands of the Provost Marshal and military police. The night before his arrival at the DTC the blue light of acetylene torches reinforcing a cage lit up the camp. There was a row of such cages.

4

The Disciplinary Training Center was a barbed-wire stockade
outside Pisa on the road to Viareggio. In it were the killers, brawl-
ers, rapists, and malingerers from line and service outfits, delivered there for rehabilitation, federal prisons at home, or the gal-
lows at Aversa. Pound was the only civilian prisoner. He was given
an Army fatigue uniform to wear, a fatigue cap, G.I. shoes and
socks. Belts and shoelaces were withheld from caged prisoners.
The following notes were made by Pound's counsel at their first
meeting in the District of Columbia jail, November 20:

At Pisa, Pound was confined in a cage made of air-strip, and in solitary confinement. Cage was in yard with little shelter from sun or rain.
Bright lights on stockade shone at night. Two guards outside at all
times. Slept on cement floor with six blankets. Can for toilet. Allowed
no reading matter except Confucius he was working on. Incommunicado. Was told nobody knew where he was.

After 3 weeks, Pound collapsed. Taken out of cage and put in tent.
Partial amnesia. Claustrophobia. Not allowed to talk to other prisoners
(told this was ordered by Washington).

No communication with outside until Oct. 3 when saw wife. No letters in or out. No recreation. Little reading matter. Suffered hysteria
and terror. Spoke only to Negro attendant who brought food.

Visit from daughter Oct. 17 and wife Nov. 3.

The tent to which he was taken was in the medical compound.
In it were a cot and a small packing crate. He went on sick call
after the other "trainees."

The pattern of the past—in Kensington, Paris, and Rapallo—
and the future in St. Elizabeths is apparent in the DTC. Word
spread that Pound had made a dummy of the camp psychiatrist.
He became a "character." He made friends. One of them was a
twenty-year-old medic named John J. Gruesen, who admired the
philosopher George Santayana and hoped to see him on a visit to
Rome. He took along Pound's regards. Santayana was shocked

to learn about Pound's confinement, and expressed admiration for
him as a poet and for his role as a "poor man's Maecenas." He
hoped that Pound would be judged as a poet, artist, and helper
of artists, and that his "confusing entry into alien disciplines
would be understood and forgiven." Pound was delighted to learn
that Santayana was well and had had a kind word for him.

There was a typewriter in the dispensary, which he was permitted to use late at night. According to Gruesen, Pound wrote
letters for some of the soldiers; several, he said, were farewell letters before an execution.

It was on this typewriter that Pound worked on *The Pisan
Cantos,* accompanying his typing with a high-pitched humming.
Environment and memories constitute the poem:

> And there was a smell of mint under the tent flaps
> especially after the rain. . . .

but later that year:

> If the hoar frost grip thy tent
> Thou wilt give thanks when night is spent.

The crate on which he wrote his drafts:

> (O Mercury god of thieves, your caduceus
> is now used by the american army
>   as witness this packing case).

A fellow prisoner made him a present:

>   "doan you tell no one
> I made you that table."

He recalled his youth in Pennsylvania, his college days in Clinton, New York, his sojourn in England, and the friends who had
gone off to another war, the Great War of 1914–1918. Of himself
at that time he wrote (grace notes to "Hugh Selwyn Mauberley"?):

> and a navvy rolls up to me in Church St. (Kensington End) with
>   Yurra Jurrmun!
> To which I replied: I am *not.*
> "Well yurr szum kind ov a furriner."

Of Churchill's defeat at the polls:

>   Oh to be in England now that Winston's out
>   Now that there's room for doubt
>   And the bank may be the nation's. . . .

He grieved for Mussolini:

>   and as to poor old Benito
>   one had a safety-pin
>   one had a bit of string, one had a button
>   all of them so far beneath him
>   half-baked and amateur
>   or mere scoundrels. . . .

He grieved for himself:

>   Tard, très tard je t'ai connue, la Tristesse,
>   I have been hard as youth sixty years

and

>   Oh let an old man rest.

When he made an error in typing, according to Robert L. Allen, another G.I., Pound swore "well and profusely." To all the medics on duty he talked about "dunghill usurers" and "usuring cutthroats," about the American people "swindled on monetary exchanges," and sometimes asked: "When will the United States return to Constitutional government?"

5

The war in the Pacific was over. Replacement personnel arrived in the Theaters of Operation in Europe. From time to time, in the Peninsula Base Section which had jurisdiction over him, questions were asked about the civilian prisoner under medical care in the DTC at Pisa. A decision was reached at the highest level.

October 22, 1945

TO FOR ACTION: AGWAR

SIGNED: COMGENMED

EZRA POUND, American expatriate in ITALY, indicted 1942 [read 1943] for TREASON, has been in Military custody since May 1945 while FBI Agents investigated the case.

All FBI Agents will have departed for the UNITED STATES by end of October.

No instructions for disposal of POUND have been received from either the War Department or the Department of Justice.

Urgently desired is information concerning disposal of subject otherwise this Theater will release him.

The message originated with G–2, but there were other interested branches, in particular the Judge Advocate General's, which noted the action taken and then drafted a message of its own for the Peninsula Base Section's commanding officer, duly sent.

October 30, 1945

TO FOR ACTION: CG, PBS FOR G–1

SIGNED: COMGENMED

WASHINGTON has been requested to advise disposition desired of POUND. Until further instructions from this Headquarters POUND will remain in present confinement.

The day was Pound's sixtieth birthday. He did not know of the renewed interest in his case until he read, in the Mediterranean edition of *Stars and Stripes,* that several Italian radio technicians and announcers were being flown to Washington to testify against him. And now, from the Office of the Judge Advocate General War Crimes Office in that city, came the long-awaited instructions.

November 5, 1945

FROM: AGWAR

TO: COMGENMED

For Theater Judge Advocate

The Department of Justice shortly will ask for return to the UNITED STATES of EZRA POUND, 14 November probable target date. We will give you about 3 days notice of date for POUND's arrival here. Legal Jurisdiction requires that plane returning prisoner land at Bolling Field in the

District of Columbia and NOT at National Airport or other airports in the UNITED STATES.

Arrangements to be made here for relinquishing POUND to Federal Bureau of Investigation upon arrival at Bolling Field.

Advise this office of destination of plane and time of departure of 6 Italian witnesses in EZRA POUND case.

November 16, 1945
FROM: AGWAR FROM SERVJAG
TO: COMGENMED

Return of EZRA POUND is subject.

Secretary of War directs that ATC pick up POUND on highest priority on regular flight leaving ROME 17 November and arriving US 19 November.

POUND is to be transported under military guards until relinquishment to federal authorities in US.

Most important that first landing of plane must be at Bolling Field in District of Columbia and NO other.

Advise ATC to communicate their Headquarters WASHINGTON of plane designation and probable time of arrival at Bolling Field.

Request immediate reply.

The emphasis placed on where the plane bearing Pound was to land is further explained in a memorandum from the Judge Advocate General's office to the Commanding General of the Air Transport Command, sent the same day:

Inasmuch as jurisdiction over crimes committed outside the United States is in the district in which the defendant is found or first brought, it is of the utmost importance that Pound be brought directly to the District of Columbia, and that the plane carrying him should not make any landing in the United States prior to its arrival at Bolling Field. It is understood that normally this flight stops at LaGuardia Field and at National Airport. It is especially desired that this be not done in this instance and that the first landing in the United States be at Bolling Field, D.C.

In the event that a forced landing is necessary before Bolling Field is reached, custody over Pound is to be retained by military authorities until he can be released to officials of the Department of Justice in the District of Columbia.

6

Pound was in the DTC dispensary, reading Joseph E. Davies'
Mission to Moscow, when two young lieutenants entered and told
him he was to be flown to Washington and to get his things together. He handed the book to the charge of quarters and asked
him to thank all the medics for him. The trip to Rome was made
by jeep. It was night when his plane arrived in Washington,
Sunday, November 18. He was taken to the District of Columbia
jail where, in 1942, six Nazi saboteurs had been executed. The
next day he was brought before Chief Judge Bolitha J. Laws. He
was still wearing his DTC clothes, a soiled G.I. sweatshirt under
his coat, baggy trousers, and oversize G.I. shoes. He asked permission to act as his own counsel, but was told the charge was too
serious for that. Judge Laws set November 27 for a formal arraignment, and Pound was taken back to the District jail. He did
not see his counsel until the following day.

On November 23 he was taken in a police van to the "bull pen"
in the courthouse, where he was kept all day, with other prisoners.
The grand jury was sitting that day to indict him anew. On November 24 and 25 he was kept locked in his cell, as were other
prisoners, because of a jail break. He suffered extremely from
claustrophobia, and spent the night of the 25th in the jail infirmary.

The second indictment, handed up on the 26th, superseded the
first. Many of the specifications now contained the names of Italian radio technicians, two witnesses being required by law in a
case of treason. The technicians had been flown to the United
States to testify before the grand jury.

Pound said in Genoa: "If I ain't worth more alive than dead,
that's that. If a man isn't willing to take some risk for his opinions,
either his opinions are no good or he's no good." In Washington
he asked: "Does anyone know what I really said?" The superseding
indictment offered answers. Neither he nor his counsel had seen it
when he was arraigned the following day.

The Grand Jurors for the United States of America duly impaneled and sworn in the District Court of the United States for the District of Columbia and inquiring for that District upon their oath present;

1. That Ezra Pound, the defendant herein, was born at Hailey, Idaho, October 30, 1885, and that he has been at all times herein mentioned and now is a citizen of the United States of America and a person owing allegiance to the United States of America.

2. That the defendant, Ezra Pound, at Rome, Italy, and other places within the Kingdom of Italy and outside the jurisdiction of any particular state or district, but within the jurisdiction of the United States and of this Court, the District of Columbia being the district in which he was found and into which he was first brought, continuously, and at all times beginning on the 11th day of December 1941, and continuing thereafter to and including the 3rd day of May 1945, under the circumstances and conditions and in the manner and by the means hereinafter set forth, then and there being a citizen of the United States, and a person owing allegiance to the United States, in violation of said duty of allegiance, knowingly, intentionally, wilfully, unlawfully, feloniously, traitorously and treasonably did adhere to the enemies of the United States, to wit; the Kingdom of Italy and the military allies of the said Kingdom of Italy, with which the United States at all times since December 11, 1941, and during the times set forth in this indictment, have been at war, giving to the said enemies of the United States aid and comfort within the United States and elsewhere, that is to say:

3. That the aforesaid adherence of the said defendant, Ezra Pound, to the Kingdom of Italy and its military allies and the giving of aid and comfort by the said defendant, Ezra Pound, to the aforesaid enemies of the United States during the time aforesaid consisted:

(a) Of accepting employment from the Kingdom of Italy in the capacity of a radio propagandist and in the performance of the duties thereof which involved the composition of texts, speeches, talks and announcements and the recording thereof for subsequent broadcast over short-wave radio on wave lengths audible in the United States and elsewhere on ordinary commercial radio receiving sets having short-wave reception facilities; and

(b) Of counselling and aiding the Kingdom of Italy and its military allies and proposing and advocating to the officials of the Government of the Kingdom of Italy ideas and thoughts, as well as methods by which such ideas and thoughts could be disseminated, which the said defendant, Ezra Pound, believed suitable and useful to the Kingdom of Italy for propaganda purposes in the prosecution of said war;

That the aforesaid activities of the said defendant, Ezra Pound, were intended to persuade citizens and residents of the United States to decline to support the United States in the conduct of the said war, to weaken or destroy confidence in the Government of the United States and in the integrity and loyalty of the Allies of the United States, and to further bind together and increase the morale of the subjects of the Kingdom of Italy in support of the prosecution of the said war by the Kingdom of Italy and its military allies.

4. And the Grand Jurors aforesaid upon their oath aforesaid do further present that the said defendant, Ezra Pound, in the prosecution, performance and execution of said treason and of said unlawful, traitorous and treasonable adhering and giving aid and comfort to the enemies of the United States, at the several times hereinafter set forth in the specifications hereof (being times when the United States were at war with the Kingdom of Italy and its military allies), unlawfully, feloniously, wilfully, knowingly, traitorously and treasonably and with intent to adhere to and give aid and comfort to the said enemies, did do, perform, and commit certain overt and manifest acts, that is to say:

1. On or about September 11, 1942, the said defendant, Ezra Pound, for the purpose of giving aid and comfort to the Kingdom of Italy and its then allies in the war against the United States, spoke into a microphone at a radio station in Rome, Italy, controlled by the Italian Government, and thereby recorded and caused to be recorded certain messages, speeches and talks for subsequent broadcast to the United States and its military allies; that the purpose of said messages, speeches and talks was, among other things, to create dissension and distrust between the United States and its military allies; and that in said speeches, messages and talks the said defendant asserted, in substance, that the war is an economic war in which the United States and its allies are the aggressors.

2. On or about December 10, 1942, the said defendant, Ezra Pound, for the purpose of giving aid and comfort to the Kingdom of Italy and its then allies in the war against the United States, spoke into a microphone at a radio station in Rome, Italy, controlled by the Italian Government, and thereby recorded and caused to be recorded certain messages, speeches and talks for subsequent broadcast to the United States and its military allies, and that the purport of said messages, speeches and talks was to create racial prejudice in the United States.

3. On or about February 4, 1943, the said defendant, Ezra Pound, for

the purpose of giving aid and comfort to the Kingdom of Italy and its then allies in the war against the United States, spoke into a microphone at a radio station in Rome, Italy, controlled by the Italian Government, and thereby recorded and caused to be recorded certain messages, speeches and talks for subsequent broadcast to the United States and its military allies.

4. On March 19, 1943, the said defendant, Ezra Pound, for the purpose of giving aid and comfort to the Kingdom of Italy and its then allies in the war against the United States, spoke into a microphone at a radio station in Rome, Italy, controlled by the Italian Government and thereby recorded and caused to be recorded certain messages, speeches and talks for subsequent broadcast to the United States and its military allies, and that the purpose of said messages, speeches and talks was, among other things, to cause dissension and distrust between the United States and England and Russia.

5. On or about May 12, 1943, the said defendant, Ezra Pound, for the purpose of giving aid and comfort to the Kingdom of Italy and its then allies in the war against the United States, spoke into a microphone at a radio station in Rome, Italy, controlled by the Italian Government and thereby recorded and caused to be recorded certain messages, speeches and talks for subsequent broadcast to the United States and its military allies, and that in said messages, speeches and talks the said defendant asserted, among other things and in substance, that Italy is the natural ally of the United States; that the true nature of the Axis regime has been misrepresented to the people in the United States and that England, Russia and the United States are aggressor nations.

6. On or about May 14, 1943, the said defendant, Ezra Pound, for the purpose of giving aid and comfort to the Kingdom of Italy and its then allies in the war against the United States, spoke into a microphone at a radio station in Rome, Italy, controlled by the Italian Government and thereby recorded and caused to be recorded certain messages, speeches and talks for subsequent broadcast to the United States and its military allies, and that the purport of said messages, speeches and talks was to create racial prejudice and distrust of the Government of the United States.

7. On or about May 15, 1943, the said defendant, Ezra Pound, for the purpose of giving aid and comfort to the Kingdom of Italy and its then allies in the war against the United States, spoke into a microphone at a radio station in Rome, Italy, controlled by the Italian Government and thereby recorded and caused to be recorded certain messages,

speeches and talks for subsequent broadcast to the United States and
its military allies, and that in said messages, speeches and talks the said
defendant praised Italy, urged the people in the United States to read
European publications rather than the American press and to listen to
European radio transmissions, and stated further that he spoke "from
Rome, in a regime where liberty is considered a duty. . . ."

8. Between July 29, 1942 and July 25, 1943, the said defendant, Ezra
Pound, for the purpose of giving aid and comfort to the Kingdom of
Italy and its then allies in the war against the United States, on a day
and date to these Grand Jurors unknown, and in the presence of
Armando Giovagnoli and Giuseppe Bruni, spoke into a microphone in
a radio station at Rome, Italy, controlled by the Italian Government
and thereby recorded and caused to be recorded certain messages,
speeches and talks for subsequent broadcast to the United States and its
military allies.

9. Between July 29, 1942 and July 25, 1943, the said defendant, Ezra
Pound, for the purpose of giving aid and comfort to the Kingdom of
Italy and its then allies in the war against the United States, on a day
and date to these Grand Jurors unknown, and in the presence of
Armando Giovagnoli and Fernando de Leonardis, spoke into a microphone in a radio station at Rome, Italy, controlled by the Italian Government and thereby recorded and caused to be recorded certain messages, speeches and talks for subsequent broadcast to the United States
and its military allies.

10. Between August 22, 1942 and July 25, 1943, the said defendant,
Ezra Pound, for the purpose of giving aid and comfort to the Kingdom
of Italy and its then allies in the war against the United States, on a day
and date to these Grand Jurors unknown, and in the presence of Walter
Zanchetti and Giuseppe Bruni, spoke into a microphone in a radio station at Rome, Italy, controlled by the Italian Government and thereby
recorded and caused to be recorded certain messages, speeches and talks
for subsequent broadcast to the United States and its military allies.

11. Between August 22, 1942 and July 25, 1943, the said defendant,
Ezra Pound, for the purpose of giving aid and comfort to the Kingdom
of Italy and its then allies in the war against the United States, on a day
and date to these Grand Jurors unknown, and in the presence of Walter
Zanchetti and Fernando de Leonardis, spoke into a microphone in a
radio station in Rome, Italy, controlled by the Italian Government and
thereby recorded and caused to be recorded certain messages, speeches

and talks for subsequent broadcast to the United States and its military allies.

12. Between December 11, 1941 and July 25, 1943, the said defendant, Ezra Pound, for the purpose of giving aid and comfort to the Kingdom of Italy and its then allies in the war against the United States, on a day and date to these Grand Jurors unknown, and in the presence of Fernando Luzzi and Giuseppe Bruni, spoke into a microphone in a radio station at Rome, Italy, controlled by the Italian Government and thereby recorded and caused to be recorded certain messages, speeches and talks for subsequent broadcast to the United States and its military allies.

13. Between December 11, 1941 and July 25, 1943, the said defendant, Ezra Pound, for the purpose of giving aid and comfort to the Kingdom of Italy and its then allies in the war against the United States, on a day and date to these Grand Jurors unknown, and in the presence of Fernando Luzzi and Giuseppe Bruni, spoke into a microphone in a radio station at Rome, Italy, controlled by the Italian Government and thereby recorded and caused to be recorded certain messages, speeches and talks for subsequent broadcast to the United States and its military allies [*sic*].

14. Between December 11, 1941 and July 25, 1943, the said defendant, Ezra Pound, for the purpose of giving aid and comfort to the Kingdom of Italy and its then allies in the war against the United States, on a day and date to these Grand Jurors unknown, and in the presence of Giuseppe Bruni and Fernando de Leonardis, spoke into a microphone in a radio station at Rome, Italy, controlled by the Italian Government and thereby recorded and caused to be recorded certain messages, speeches and talks for subsequent broadcast to the United States and its military allies.

15. Between April 1, 1942 and July 23, 1943, the said defendant, Ezra Pound, for the purpose of giving aid and comfort to the Kingdom of Italy and its then allies in the war against the United States, on a day and date to these Grand Jurors unknown, conferred and counselled with Salvatore Aponte and Adriano Ungaro, officials of the Ministry of Popular Culture of the Kingdom of Italy, for the purpose of securing their approval of manuscripts composed by said defendant to be used in the making of recordings for subsequent broadcast to the United States and elsewhere.

16. On or about July 11, 1942, the said defendant, Ezra Pound, for

the purpose of giving aid and comfort to the Kingdom of Italy and its then allies in the war against the United States, accepted and received payment and remuneration in the sum of 700 liras from the Kingdom of Italy for compiling and recording messages, speeches and talks for subsequent broadcast to the United States and elsewhere from a radio station in Rome, Italy.

17. Between December 11, 1941 and May 3, 1945, the said defendant, Ezra Pound, for the purpose of giving aid and comfort to the Kingdom of Italy and its then allies in the war against the United States, on a day and date to these Grand Jurors unknown, accepted and received payment and remuneration from the Kingdom of Italy in an amount to these Grand Jurors unknown, for compiling and recording messages, speeches and talks from subsequent broadcast to the United States and elsewhere from a radio station in Rome, Italy.

18. On or about June 24, 1942, the said defendant, Ezra Pound, for the purpose of giving aid and comfort to the Kingdom of Italy and its then allies in the war against the United States, accepted and received payment and remuneration in the sum of 350 liras, from the Kingdom of Italy for compilation of notes and comments for broadcast to the United States and elsewhere from a radio station located in the Kingdom of Italy.

19. Between December 11, 1941 and May 3, 1945, the said defendant, Ezra Pound, for the purpose of giving aid and comfort to the Kingdom of Italy and its then allies in the war against the United States, on a day and date to these Grand Jurors unknown, accepted and received payment and remuneration from the Kingdom of Italy in an amount to these Grand Jurors unknown, for compilation of notes and comments for broadcast to the United States and elsewhere from a radio station located in the Kingdom of Italy.

The defendant, Ezra Pound, committed each and every one of the overt acts herein described for the purpose of, and with the intent to adhere to and give aid and comfort to the Kingdom of Italy, and its military allies, enemies of the United States, and the said defendant, Ezra Pound, committed each and every one of the said overt acts contrary to his duty of allegiance to the United States and to the form of the statute and constitution in such case made and provided and against the peace and dignity of the United States. (Section 1, United States Criminal Code.)

seven

Points of View

E. E. CUMMINGS

Re Ezra Pound—poetry happens to be an art; and artists happen to be human beings.

An artist doesn't live in some geographical abstraction, super-imposed on a part of this beautiful earth by the nonimagination of unanimals and dedicated to the proposition that massacre is a social virtue because murder is an individual vice. Nor does an artist live in some soi-disant world, nor does he live in some so-called universe, nor does he live in any number of "worlds" or in any number of "universes." As for a few trifling delusions like the "past" and "present" and "future" of quote mankind un-quote, they may be big enough for a couple of billion super-mechanized submorons but they're much too small for one human being.

Every artist's strictly illimitable country is himself.

An artist who plays that country false has committed suicide;

and even a good lawyer cannot kill the dead. But a human being who's true to himself—whoever himself may be—is immortal; and all the atomic bombs of all the antiartists in spacetime will never civilize immortality.

WILLIAM CARLOS WILLIAMS

I can't write about Ezra Pound with any sort of composure. When I think of the callousness of some of his letters during the last six or seven years, blithe comments touching "fresh meat on the Russian steppes" or the war in Spain as being of "no more importance than the draining of some mosquito swamp in deepest Africa," "Hitler the martyr" and all that—I want to forget that I ever knew him. His vicious anti-Semitism and much else have lowered him in my mind further than I ever thought it possible to lower a man whom I had once admired. But that isn't the whole story.

Somehow I am compelled to think of something I once heard about a poet during one of the former Mexican revolutions. This poor guy seeing the men with guns coming down the street shinnied up a telegraph pole—the only thing available to give him any elevation under the circumstances. The troops seeing him up there thought they might as well take a few pot-shots at him—anyhow it was in enemy territory. But at this the man up the pole started to yell, I'm a poet! I'm a poet! The soldiers at that invited him down, gave him a drink and told him to go ahead, poetize for them. Maybe they shot him later, I don't know.

Ezra Pound is one of the most competent poets in our language, possessed of the most acute ear for metrical sequences, to the point of genius, that we have ever known. He is also, it must be confessed, the biggest damn fool and faker in the business. You can't allow yourself to be too serious about a person like that— and yet he is important. He knows all this and plays on it to perfection.

One trait I always held against Ezra was that he'd never let you in on his personal affairs; close as we were for several years when we were kids I just never knew what he was up to. It didn't make really much difference but in a pal it was annoying. Never explain anything, was his motto. He carried it off well—and in his verse too, later. The purpose was to impress everyone about him with the profundity of his wit. I know the answer now and it isn't flattering. Generally speaking his head was fairly empty.

But he always felt himself superior to anyone about him and could never brook a rival. We accepted it on terms he little suspected, for after all he was and remains, in his field, a genius. He just lived on a different plane from anyone else in the world, a higher plane! This gave him certain prerogatives. If he was your friend you just forgave it. We were friends.

I think this trait or whatever it was bred from—if not plain emptiness—is the thing that finally ruined Ezra. He tried to make good and with better financial success in his field might have done so—but he was a lazy animal in many ways and couldn't be bothered. We had a chronic argument going on between us, he and I, over which was the proper objective for the writer, caviar or bread. I held out for bread, Ezra for caviar. This went on for years. Finally one day I got a letter from London saying: bread.

But that was only a momentary aberration on the part of the grrrrrrreatest poet drawing breath in our day! And he meant it. That was no joke to Ezra. He really lived the poet as few of us had the nerve to live that exalted reality in our time. As always the details are best omitted, they were part of the aura.

I remember one April morning in 1909 we were passing a church in Kensington with a high, spiked iron fence around it. On the pavement before us lay a very much battered bunch of violets dropped no doubt by some child or lady. After a step or two Ezra stopped, turned back, raised the flowers with a great show from their neglected position and placed them honored upon the iron fence-rail. We moved on, he insisting on being one step in advance of me as always. I remember my brother once in the same situation turned and walked off in the opposite direction.

I say these things because I can't help saying them—they are part of the Ezra Pound I knew, the man now in jeopardy of his life as a traitor to his country. Ezra always insisted, in the loudest terms, on the brilliance and profundity of his mind. He doesn't have a great mind and never did but that doesn't make him any the less a good poet. His stupidities coupled with his overweening self-esteem have brought him down—but to try to make a criminal of him because of that is to lay ourselves open to the accusation of being moved by an even greater stupidity than that which we are facing. There are plenty of others in his category with far less talent.

Ezra is one of a well recognized group of Americans who can't take the democratic virus and stand up under it, very distinguished men most of them who owe their distinction largely to their American origins. They owe their overall genius, of course, to their immediate ancestry, such traits as appeared both in William and Henry James. But with the artist, and we are speaking of the artist in this case, the distinguishing genus of their characteristics has been definitely the environment, the fact of their new world origins—from which they recoil.

Pitiful to relate, revulsion is invariably the type of reaction they suffer. No use to go into further detail, it is common. And I for one believe that had they remained nearer to the fountain which gave them originally their power to go abroad and develop their traits, even in the case of Henry James—their work would have assumed more impressive proportions. Nor am I blind to the knowledge that had they not gone abroad, they might have perished. I think they could have lived it out here somehow without perishing. Let that pass.

Ezra Pound the consummate poet taken as any sort of menace to America when compared with some of the vicious minds at large among us in, say for instance the newspaper game, as well as other rackets which have the public ear, is sheer childishness. He just isn't dangerous, they are. I am not trying to minimize his crime, it was a crime and he committed it wilfully. But under the circumstances and knowing what goes on "in committee" and elsewhere in our magnificently destined country—I don't think we should be too hard on him. I have thought, in spite of his infantile mental pattern, and still think—knowing what goes on about me every day as reported in the drivel of the press—that as a poet Ezra

Pound at Hamilton College, 1905 [*From a photograph of the poet at twenty, now in the Humanities Research Center Library, University of Texas*]

A pride of poets, January 18, 1914. Place: "Newbuildings," home of Wilfred Scawen Blunt. Occasion: a dinner. Main course: roasted peacock. Left to right: Victor Plarr, Sturge Moore, William Butler Yeats, Blunt, Ezra Pound, Richard Aldington, F. S. Flint [*Humanities Research Center Library*]

The middle period [*A signed photograph from the Humanities Research Center Library*]

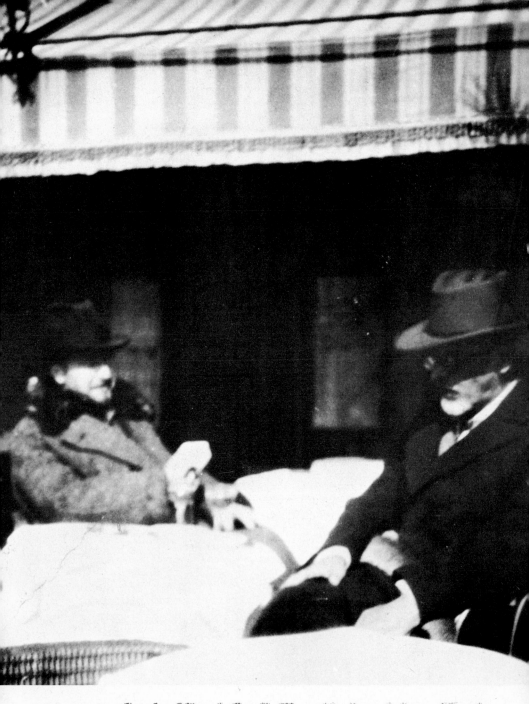

Pound and Yeats in Rapallo [*Humanities Research Center Library*]

The broadcaster: Pound in front of his Rome hotel, 1941 [*Wide World*]

ABOVE: Row of security cages at D. T. C., with prisoners. A corner of Pound's cage, specially made of airstrip steel, is at the extreme left [*Signal Corps photo*]

BELOW: Pound in Security cage No. 1
[*On-the-spot sketch from the collection of H. A. Sieber*]

Pound arrives in Washington after flight from Italy, 1945, in custody of U. S. marshals [*Wide World*]

IN THE HOUSE OF REPRESENTATIVES

AUGUST 21, 1957

Mr. BURDICK submitted the following resolution; which was referred to the Committee on Rules

RESOLUTION

Whereas Ezra Pound has been incarcerated in Saint Elizabeths Hospital for the past twelve years on the assumption that he is insane; and

Whereas many people visit him there and are convinced that he is not insane: Therefore be it

1 *Resolved,* That the Committee on the Judiciary, acting
2 as a whole or by subcommittee, is authorized and directed
3 to conduct a full and complete investigation and study of
4 the sanity of Ezra Pound, in order to determine whether
5 there is justification for his continued incarceration in Saint
6 Elizabeths Hospital.

7 For the purpose of carrying out this resolution the com-
8 mittee or subcommittee is authorized to sit and act during the

1 present Congress at such times and places within the United
2 States, whether the House is in session, has recessed, or has
3 adjourned, to hold such hearings, and to require, by subpena
4 or otherwise, the attendance and testimony of such witnesses
5 and the production of such books, records, correspondence,
6 memorandums, papers, and documents, as it deems necessary;
7 except that neither the committee nor any subcommittee
8 thereof may sit while the House is meeting unless special
9 leave to sit shall have been obtained from the House. Sub-
10 penas may be issued under the signature of the chairman of
11 the committee or any member of the committee designated
12 by him, and may be served by any person designated by
13 such chairman or member.

14 The committee shall report to the House on or before
15 the first day of the second session of the present Congress the
16 results of its investigation and study, together with such
17 recommendations as it deems advisable. Any such report
18 which is made when the House is not in session shall be filed
19 with the Clerk of the House.

85TH CONGRESS
1ST SESSION

H. RES. 403

RESOLUTION

To authorize the Committee on the Judiciary to conduct an investigation of the sanity of Ezra Pound.

By Mr. BURDICK

AUGUST 21, 1957
Referred to the Committee on Rules

The House Resolution submitted by Rep. Usher L. Burdick, which paved the way for Pound's release

Pound outside the courthouse after dismissal of the indictment, April 18, 1958 [*Wide World*]

Pound at the home of Rep. Burdick. With them is H. A. Sieber, author of Congressional report on Pound case [*From* The Washington Star *of April 29, 1958*]

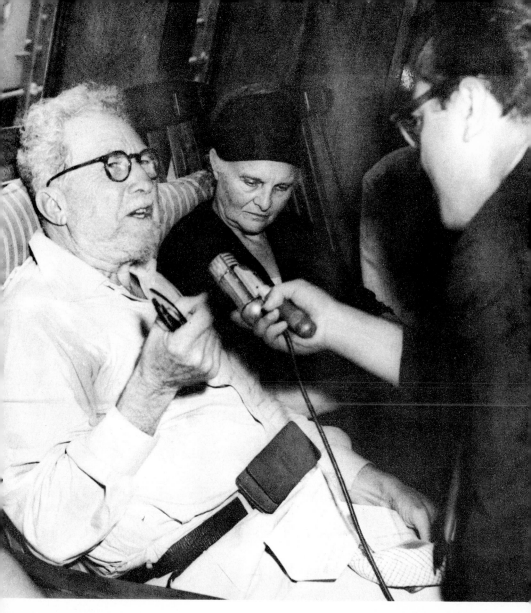

Pound and his wife on board the *Cristoforo Colombo* en route to Italy [*Italian Line photograph, courtesy H. A. Sieber*]

A recent photograph [*Humanities Research Center Library*]

had some sort of right to speak his mind, such as it had become, as he did.

I have to qualify the above paragraph, however, by saying that I never heard a word that Ezra Pound broadcast during the war from Italy. The only thing I know directly about his broadcasts is a single sentence, referring to myself, which one of the tellers in our bank told my wife one morning more than a year ago. From the quality of that I judge of the rest, dull stuff.

When they lock the man up with Jim and John and Henry and Mary and Dolores and Grace—I hope they will give him access to books, with paper enough, for him to go on making translations for us from the classics such as we have never seen except at his hands in our language.

It would be the greatest miscarriage of justice, human justice, to shoot him.

LOUIS ZUKOFSKY

I should prefer to say nothing now. But a preference for silence might be misinterpreted by even the closest friends.

When he was here in 1939, I told him that I did not doubt his integrity had decided his political action, but I pointed to his head, indicating something had gone wrong. When he asked me if it was possible to educate certain politicians, I retorted, Whatever you don't know, Ezra, you ought to know *voices*. This exchange of frankness was accepted tacitly by both of us as a dissociation of values above personal bickering.

He approached literature and music at that depth. His profound and intimate knowledge and practice of these things still leave that part of his mind entire. The heavy-footed will never see the truth of his essay "Mediaevilism" or know the worth of Canto I or Canto XIII, or of—

> Sun up; work
> Sundown; to rest
> dig well and drink of the water
> dig field; eat of the grain

> Imperial power is? And to us what is it?
> The fourth; the dimension of stillness.
> And the power over wild beasts.

Or the weight of "Anyone can run to excesses," or the fact of "Who even dead, yet hath his mind entire."

I never felt the least trace of anti-Semitism in his presence. Nothing he ever said to me made me feel the embarrassment I always have for the "Goy" in whom a residue of antagonism to "Jew" remains. If we had occasion to use the words "Jew" and "Goy" they were no more or less ethnological in their sense than "Chinese" and "Italian."

I remember an animated cartoon which pointed up human brutishness over which both of us could still chuckle. He may be condemned or forgiven. Biographers of the future may find his character as charming a subject as that of Aaron Burr. It will matter very little against his finest work overshadowed in his lifetime by the hell of Belsen which he overlooked.

F. O. MATTHIESSEN

In considering the case of Ezra Pound, one must never forget his important role in the poetic renaissance of 30 years ago. That importance may finally have consisted more in his critical stimulus and instigation than in his own work, although he was hailed as a master craftsman by no less than both Yeats and Eliot. In this country, Harriet Monroe, the editor of *Poetry,* declared that "it was due more to Ezra Pound than to any other person that 'the revolution' was on." And when that revolution was still new, Carl Sandburg added: "He has done most of living men to incite new impulses in poetry."

But Pound cannot be considered as a poet withdrawn from the world, like Emily Dickinson or Rilke, for instance. From the familiar position of the Bohemian artist who felt it his duty to thumb his nose at the bourgeois, he advanced at the time of the depression to an active concern with economics and politics. He did not want to be regarded as an irresponsible, although his political tracts, such as *Jefferson and/or Mussolini,* were a fantastic mixture of social credit and a literary man's admiration for the efficiency of the new Italian state.

He believed the control of money to be the central issue for any society, and he wanted his views to prevail. Throughout the 1930s he continued to bombard some members of the U.S. Congress with quotations on the monetary question from Jefferson, John Adams and others, whom he thought to have anticipated social credit. He declared more than once that Van Buren's stand on the Bank had made him one of the greatest men in our history.

The few people who read his economic tracts must have regarded him as a crackpot, and he certainly had no influence. Nor do I believe that his radio broadcasts before and after our entry into the war, vicious as they were in their anti-Semitism, could have had any ponderable force as propaganda. Pound's way of conjuring up the international Jewish bankers as a scape-goat was far too odd and literary.

Nevertheless, he took his stand on such doctrines. If art is one of the most valuable products of a civilization, then the poet must be judged for the humanity of his thought as well as for his form. And if you believe in the artist's responsibility for his views, I don't see how you can explain Pound's away. But he is a tragic instance of the consequence resulting from the gulf between poet and audience, which has been so symptomatic of recent social disequilibrium. Living for so many years as an isolated expatriate in Rapallo, Pound was so cut off from any normal contacts with society that when he began to develop a political and social theory it could only be eccentric. As an eccentric he must now be judged.

CONRAD AIKEN

I am glad you are doing a piece on Pound. For his tragic predicament he has of course only himself to blame, and like anyone else in the same situation he must alone take the consequences. That he knew this he made quite apparent on his arrest, when he remarked that if a man values his beliefs he values them enough to die for them, and if they are worth having at all they are worth the speaking out. In my opinion Pound is less traitor than fool:

his political infatuations or obsessions led him by insensible degrees across international borders; the internationalism that always marked his poetry began increasingly to stamp his political thinking; and now he finds himself under charge of treason for having, according to his own queer lights, betrayed a particular society of men for man in the abstract.

But whatever the United States government decides to be justice in his case as traitor, I think we must all see to it that justice should be done to him also as poet. He was a poet, perhaps a great one, long before he became a Fascist, he is still that poet, and one of the great creative influences of our time, and we must not permit these facts, nor his work, to be forgotten. It is for this reason that recently, when the editors of Random House refused to print Pound's poems in an anthology, or to be more exact in a new edition of that anthology, I was moved to protest. It seemed to me that a burning of the books was a kind of intellectual and moral suicide which we might more wisely leave to our enemies.

SAXE COMMINS, Random House editor

(Orally)

Random House is not going to publish any Fascist. As a matter of fact, we don't think that Ezra Pound is good enough, or important enough, to include. If we thought he was, we might have carried him anyway. We just don't think he is.

(By mail)

I am sending you herewith a copy of the note which will appear on Page 788 of our forthcoming Modern Library Giant volume, *An Anthology of Famous English and American Poetry*, edited by William Rose Benét and Conrad Aiken.

At this point Conrad Aiken included in the Modern Library edition of his anthology, on which the present text is based, the following poems by Ezra Pound: *Envoi (1919)*, *The Tree*, *The Tomb at Akr Caar*, *Portrait d'une Femme*, *Apparuit*, *A Virginal*, *The Return*, *The River Merchant's Wife*, *The Flame*, *Dance Figure*, *Lament of the Frontier Guard*, and *Taking Leave of a Friend*. When the publishers insisted on omitting these poems from the present edition, he consented upon one condition: that it be clearly stated in print that his wishes were overruled by the publishers, who flatly refused at this time to include a single line by Ezra Pound. This is a statement that the publishers are not only willing but delighted to print.

Their delight was brief. Mr. Bennett Cerf, president of Random House, took the problem to the readers of his column in the *Saturday Review of Literature* (as it was then called); an avalanche of letters descended on him, and the twelve poems were included in the next edition of the anthology.

It was in connection with this controversy that Pound's counsel cautioned Mr. Cerf against making libellous statements and Mrs. Pound commented: "EP. is not interested in the question of his sanity—but in establishing that he did NOT commit treason. The treason was in the White House, not in Rapallo—& people are beginning to see that at last."

eight

For the Defense

The task of defending Pound had been entrusted to Julien Cornell, thirty-five years old, by Shakespear & Parkyn, Pound's London solicitors, on the recommendation of James Laughlin, his American publisher.

Mr. Cornell, a Quaker, had been active in the field of civil liberties and held the belief that a world government would be better for mankind than the United Nations. He was endowed with great determination as well as idealism—his figure, which was stocky, his chin which was broad and firm, showed it. He accepted the brief in a difficult time, when the feelings aroused by his client's broadcasts were still strong; in doing so, he acted in the highest tradition of the American bar—that of safeguarding every accused man's right to his day in court. He had, in addition to conviction and courage, the professional skill needed and, like Dr. Johnson on toleration, "untwisted this difficult subject with great dexterity." He was a graduate of Swarthmore College and the Yale Law School.

Mr. Cornell saw his client for the first time on November 20 in the District of Columbia jail and jotted down the notes on Pound's ordeal in the DTC, previously given. On November 27, the day scheduled for the formal arraignment, he found Pound in a state of "almost complete" mental and physical exhaustion. He attempted to explain to Pound that he was to be arraigned and that he would have to plead to the indictment. Mr. Cornell suggested that because of his condition Pound might be wise to remain mute rather than enter a plea of "not guilty." Pound's mouth opened once or twice, but no words came. He looked up at the ceiling and his face began to twitch. He said he felt ill and asked to be returned to the infirmary.

At the arraignment later that day Mr. Cornell told Chief Judge Laws that his client was not well enough to plead, and Pound was allowed to remain mute and seated. Under the law, a plea of "not guilty" was entered by the judge. A motion for bail followed. In the end, it may be thought, bail—and private treatment—might have served justice better as well as Pound.

The government was represented by Isaiah Matlack, a Special Assistant to the Attorney General. To him, and to Judge Laws, Mr. Cornell now gave copies of two documents he had prepared; these were an affidavit in support of the motion for bail, and a memorandum of law. The gist of the affidavit was presented orally by Mr. Cornell.

"I am an attorney at law of New York and have appeared herein for the defendant, Ezra Pound, at the request of his London solicitors, and with the permission of the court, for the sole purpose of this arraignment. I do not defend his actions, nor do I approve his sentiments. I do not feel that I can properly try his case. But in accordance with my duty as a lawyer, I have felt obliged to comply with a request that I confer with this man accused of crime.

"I must report that the defendant, Ezra Pound, after his arrest on a charge of treason last May, has been continuously held incommunicado in solitary confinement, under such extreme conditions that he suffered a complete mental collapse and loss of memory. Although he has partially recovered his health, I believe that he is still insane and that if he remains in prison he may never recover, and not only will he be unable to stand trial on this indictment, but one of the greatest literary geniuses of these times will be permanently eclipsed.

"I urge this court to order his removal at once from the District of Columbia jail, where he is now confined, to a civilian mental hospital or sanatorium under bail, or that if bail is not permitted, he be removed to a civilian mental hospital or sanatorium operated by the United States and placed in custody of a civilian physician. I believe that such action is imperative, and that if it is not taken immediately, he will never recover his senses sufficiently to defend himself against the indictment which has been handed up to the court.

"This affidavit is accompanied by a memorandum of law relating to the crime charged, showing that the statutes permit the admission of the defendant to bail, although treason is a capital offense. This affidavit will be confined to the facts in the case, which are stated to the best of my information and belief, to the extent necessary for the purposes of the relief now prayed for. In order to furnish the court with further information about the defendant, if desired, I have appended as Exhibit A, a copy of the only material concerning him which has been published currently, namely, an article which appeared in the newspaper *PM* (New York) for November 25, 1945."

The biographical and literary history of Pound in the article and affidavit has been covered in the present narrative; Mr. Cornell's purpose in presenting that history was to assure Judge Laws that the defendant was not the type of man who would attempt to leave the jurisdiction of the court "while the trial is pending." The affidavit continues:

"It is not necessary to recount the story of Pound's downfall. I need only say that his extraordinary conduct, his vilification of the nation's leaders during war time, his vainglory and vituperations, his anti-Semitic and vulgar utterances, as broadcast over the Rome radio, cannot be explained on any basis of mere venality but only on the ground that Pound is an old man no longer in the full possession of his mental powers. I am led to this belief not only because the mentality of the man in his prime and the ridiculous broadcasts of his old age are utterly incompatible, but also because his intimates tell me that the evidence of mental deterioration in his private correspondence is unmistakable, and in the opinion of many of his close friends and associates his mind has been deteriorating for a number of years, far beyond mere senility or eccentricity.

"It was this streak of mental weakness in Pound, which had long been evident to his friends, that led him, I believe, into mental collapse when he was subjected to the rigors of imprisonment.

"Early in May of this year, Pound accosted the first American he saw, a Negro soldier advancing with the native *Partigiani*, by whom he was taken at his own request to an American command post at Lavagna, whence he was sent to the army's Counter Information Center at Genoa. Pound was under house arrest during this time, being treated as a political prisoner.

"After several weeks at Genoa, Pound was handcuffed and taken away by military police in a jeep, naively believing that he was bound for an airport and a plane to the United States. But his actual destination was an American military prison at Pisa.

"Here began a period of imprisonment which destroyed the poet's mind and all but killed his aging body. For this unfortunate result, the administrators of the prison should not be criticized. No doubt they treated Pound exactly as they would any other man charged with a like offense. No doubt Pound when he entered the prison appeared to be merely an eccentric, with no evidence of insanity on the surface, and no reason to suspect insanity. The fact that Pound's mind cracked after a week or so of imprisonment was nobody's fault.

"He was at once beset with fears—that he would be thrown with murderers and felons who would kill him; that nobody knew where he was and nobody would ever know what happened to him.

"Pound was placed in solitary confinement in a steel cage specially built for him in the prison yard. He knew not whether he would rot away in this cage or be taken out and hanged as a traitor.

But far worse than these was the thought that his wife and daughter would never know his fate, and would dream, until they reached their own graves, of the agony interred in his. Not far away were the pens in which long term offenders were confined, but all other prisoners were forbidden to speak to Pound, and could not come near him. Not only was the prisoner deprived of all human companionship, but he was given no reading matter to relax his fevered brain. He had nothing to employ his time but a Chinese text of Confucius which he had been translating, nothing to distract his mind from worry and fear.

"And such mental torture was not all he suffered. It was now full summer, and the Italian sun beat down on the prison yard with unbearable intensity. A military highway ran nearby, and having no shelter, he could not escape the ceaseless noise and dust. Although all the other prisoners were supplied with tents to keep out the heat and glare of the sun, Pound was given no such protection, probably so that guards could watch him at all times. Whereas other prisoners were let out of the cages for meals and exercise, Pound was always confined. While others were penned up in groups, he was alone in his cage.

"After enduring the tropical sun all day, neither sleep nor rest came with the night—electric lights glared into the poet's cage and burned into his bloodshot eyes. The cage was devoid of all furniture. Pound lay upon the cement floor in his blankets, broiled by the sun and wet by the rain.

"After about three weeks of struggle to maintain his sanity, the wretched man fell ill. The heat and the glare, added to the hopelessness of being held incommunicado and the torture of solitary confinement, were more than his aging mind could bear. Pound was stricken with violent and hysterical terror. He lost his memory. He became desperately thin and weak until finally the prison doctor feared for him.

"Pound was then taken out of his unhappy cage and placed in a tent. He was given a cot to lie upon, and medical treatment. The doctor even prescribed a walk each day, but most often the guards neglected to take him out for exercise.

"While the doctors took measures to keep Pound's body alive, his mind was not rescued. He was still kept in solitary confinement, still held incommunicado, still deprived of all reading matter but religious tracts. As physical strength gradually flowed back into his body, the terror and hysteria subsided somewhat, memory returned, but the great mind remained impaired, and fits of shuddering terror balked his struggle to regain his senses.

"The period of violent insanity apparently began about mid-June, to endure for three months or more.

"Not until October 3rd could the prisoner communicate with the outside world. On that day his wife was allowed to see him for half an hour. Two weeks later he saw his daughter for a like period, and on November 3rd his wife was again permitted to visit him. These visits helped to restore him to some outward semblance of his former self.

"A week or so ago, Pound being strong enough to travel, he was taken by jeep to Rome and thence by plane to Washington, where he arrived on November 18th, and has since remained, in the District of Columbia jail.

"I have twice seen Pound, talking with him for two hours and more on each occasion. While having no medical knowledge, one does not need to be a doctor to know at once that this man is not sane. The marvelous mind with its tremendous learning has been wrecked so horribly that all may see the sad results.

"I respectfully pray that the defendant be admitted to bail on the ground that he may be safely released without fear that he would attempt to flee the jurisdiction, and on the further ground that his release under bail is necessary in order that he may secure proper medical treatment. If the court determines that the defendant should not be admitted to bail, I urge that he be removed at once from imprisonment in a penal institution and that he be placed in the custody of one or more physicians in a civilian hospital or sanatorium operated by the United States or by the District of Columbia. Only in a normal environment, free from the drastic restraints which are necessary in penal hospitals, can he possibly recover, in my opinion; only by such medical treatment does he stand a chance of regaining his sanity even to the point where he could stand trial on this indictment.

"I am confident that a disinterested psychiatric investigation of his condition would show that such measures are imperative."

—————————————— **2** ——————————————

Mr. Cornell had succeeded in establishing Pound's background, accomplishments, recent ordeal, and present illness—with good effect, as it turned out. More difficult was his task to prove the crime of treason bailable. Precedents were rare; but admission to bail was permitted by statute in all capital offenses. Two cases— one of treason in 1795, the other piracy, 1813—appeared to fulfill certain requirements. Perhaps what made the second one interesting was the fact that the defendant was ill, and the 1813 court held that continued imprisonment would be dangerous.

Memorandum of Law on Application for Bail

This memorandum is submitted in support of the defendant's application for admission to bail pending trial on the indictment and is confined to a discussion of the law bearing upon the application, the facts being set forth in a separate affidavit of defendant's counsel, Julien Cornell.

The Indictment

The defendant was indicted at a criminal term held July, 1943, of the District Court of the United States for the District of Columbia, upon presentation of the Grand Jury of the District charging him with having committed the crime of treason in violation of Section I of the United States Criminal Code, by the transmission of certain broadcasts over a radio station at Rome, Italy, in which it is alleged that he, being a United States citizen, and owing allegiance to the United States, adhered and gave aid and counsel to an enemy state, namely, the Kingdom of Italy. The defendant having not yet been furnished with a copy of the indictment, and the full text not being available to counsel, the indictment is not here set forth.

The defendant's counsel is informed and believes that a superseding indictment has been, or will soon be requested by the Department of Justice alleging the same crime and on substantially the same grounds.

Constitutional Provisions

The crime of treason is the only crime which, because of its importance in Colonial times, was defined in the Constitution of the United States.

"Treason against the United States, shall consist only in levying War against them, or in adhering to their enemies, giving them Aid and Comfort. No Person shall be convicted of Treason unless on the Testimony of two Witnesses to the same overt Act, or on Confession in open Court." (U.S. Constitution, Art. 3, Sec. 3.)

Statutory Provisions

The definition of the crime of treason is also contained in the Criminal Code in language derived from the constitutional provision.

"(*Criminal Code, section 1.*) *Treason.* Whoever, owing allegiance to the United States, levies war against them or adheres to their enemies, giving them aid and comfort within the United States or elsewhere, is guilty of treason." (R.S. Sec. 5331; Mar. 4, 1909, c. 32, Sec. 1, 35 Stat. 1088.) (18 U.S. Code, Sec. 1.)

The punishment for treason is specified in Sec. 2 of the Criminal Code.

"Whoever is convicted of treason shall suffer death; or, at the discretion of the court, shall be imprisoned not less than five years and fined not less than $10,000, to be levied on and collected out of any or all of his property, real and personal, of which he was the owner at the time of committing such treason, any sale or conveyance to the contrary notwithstanding; and every person so convicted of treason shall, moreover, be incapable of holding any office under the United States." (R.S. Sec. 5332; Mar. 4, 1909, c. 321, Sec. 2, 35 Stat. 1088.) (18 U.S.C. Sec. 2.)

The laws of the United States have always contained certain procedural safeguards on behalf of a defendant accused of treason, which are derived from the Act of April 30, 1790, 1 Stat. 11 and include the following:

"*Copy of indictment and list of jurors and witnesses for prisoner.* When any person is indicted of treason, a copy of the indictment and a list of the jury, and of the witnesses to be produced on the trial for proving the indictment, stating the place of abode of each juror and witness, shall be delivered to him at least three entire days before he is tried for the same. When any person is indicted of any other capital offense, such copy of the indictment and list of the jurors and witnesses shall be delivered to him at least two entire days before the trial." (R.S. Sec. 1033.) (18 U.S.C. Sec. 562.)

"Counsel and witnesses for persons indicted for capital crimes. Every person who is indicted of treason or other capital crime, shall be allowed to make his full defense by counsel learned in the law; and the court before which he is tried, or some judge thereof, shall immediately, upon his request, assign to him such counsel, not exceeding two, as he may desire, and they shall have free access to him at all seasonable hours. He shall be allowed, in his defense, to make any proof that he can produce by lawful witnesses, and shall have the like process of the court to compel his witnesses to appear at his trial, as is usually granted to compel witnesses to appear on behalf of the prosecution." (R.S. Sec. 1034.) (18 U.S.C. Sec. 563.)

A still further safeguard was added by the Act of June 8, 1872, 17 Stat. 282, now contained in Sec. 287 of the Judicial Code.

"Challenges. When the offense charged is treason or a capital offense, the defendant shall be entitled to twenty and the United States to six peremptory challenges. On the trial of any other felony, the defendant shall be entitled to ten and the United States to six peremptory challenges. . . ." (28 U.S.C. Sec. 423.)

If the defendant should stand mute, or refuse to plead or answer upon his arraignment, it is provided by statute that the court shall enter a plea of not guilty on his behalf.

"Standing mute. When any person indicted for any offense against the United States, whether capital or otherwise, upon his arraignment stands mute, or refuses to plead or answer thereto, it shall be the duty of the court to enter the plea of not guilty on his behalf, in the same manner as if he had pleaded not guilty thereto." (R.S. Sec. 1032; 18 U.S.C. Sec. 564.)

Admission to bail is expressly permitted by statute in all capital offenses. (The crime of treason is a capital offense—Criminal Code Sec. 2 supra.)

"Bail may be admitted upon all arrests in criminal cases where the punishment may be death; but in such cases it shall be taken only by the Supreme Court or a circuit court,* or by a justice of the Supreme Court, a circuit judge, or a judge of a district court, who shall exercise their discretion therein, having regard to the nature and circumstance of the offense, and of the evidence, and to the usages of law." (R.S. Sec. 1016; 18 U.S.C. Sec. 597.)

"* NOTE: The term 'Circuit Court' is contained in the section as originally enacted and now applies to the district courts under Sec. 291 of the Act of March 3, 1911 (36 Stat. 1167) which abolished the Circuit Courts and transferred their powers and duties to the district courts."

Argument

A defendant accused of treason may be admitted to bail while awaiting trial within the discretion of the court.

As expressly provided in the statute set forth in full above "bail may be admitted upon all arrests in criminal cases where the punishment may be death" and bail may be taken by a district court or by a judge thereof "who shall exercise their discretion therein, having regard to the nature and circumstances of the offense and of the evidence, and to the usages of law." (18 U.S.C. Sec. 597, as made applicable to district courts by Act of March 3, 1911, 36 Stat. 1167.)

As provided by Sec. 2 of the Criminal Code, 18 U.S.C. Sec. 2, punishment for treason may be death or a fine and imprisonment at the discretion of the court. These statutes taken together expressly provide, therefore, that a defendant arrested on a charge of treason may be admitted to bail while awaiting trial, and that such bail may be taken by a district court or judge thereof, in his discretion, having regard to (1) the nature and circumstances of the offense, (2) the evidence against the defendant, and (3) usages of law. Discretion with regard to the granting of bail exists only in capital cases, as in all other cases the allowance of bail is mandatory. (18 U.S.C. 597.)

The crime of treason is so rare in our recent history that there is little precedent in the way of usage by which the court may be guided. Defendant's counsel has not had an opportunity to examine all the cases involving treason in recent years, to determine whether bail has been sought or permitted in any of them. The only treason case which has reached the United States Supreme Court in modern times is *Cramer v. U.S.* 325 U.S. 1. Although the opinions do not shed any light on the matter of bail, they may prove helpful as containing the only authoritative discussion of the crime, as well as a learned review of its history in English and American law.

It was established very early in the history of the United States that the crime of treason is bailable under the statutes. In the case of *U.S. v.*

Hamilton, 3 Dallas 17, (1795), the United States Supreme Court issued a writ of habeas corpus on the petition of a prisoner who had been arrested on the warrant of a district judge, charged with the crime of high treason, in that he aided insurrectionists by attending their meetings. The prisoner had been committed to jail without any hearing and then not only requested that he be properly arraigned, but also that he be admitted to bail. Despite the fact that the man was accused not merely of propaganda, but of actual aid to a rebellious group within the United States, the Supreme Court directed that he be admitted to bail until the trial and fixed the bail in the sum of $4,000 with two sureties for $2,000 each. In another capital case, this one involving the crime of piracy, Hon. Bushrod Washington, Associate Justice of the Supreme Court, sitting in the Circuit Court for the District of Pennsylvania, admitted the defendant to bail. (*U.S. v. Jones,* Fed. Cas. No. 15496, (1813).)

In the latter case, Justice Washington in admitting the defendant to bail in the sum of $10,000 stated that he granted bail because the defendant was ill and continued imprisonment would be harmful to him, although there was no immediate or certain danger that he would die if not released.

"As to Jones, it is proved by the physician who has attended him since February, in jail, that his health is bad, his complaint pulmonary, and that, in his opinion, confinement during the summer might so far increase his disorder as to render it ultimately dangerous. The humanity of our laws, not less than the feelings of the court, favor the liberation of a prisoner upon bail, under such circumstances. It is not necessary, in our view of the subject, that the danger which may arise from his confinement should be either immediate or certain. If, in the opinion of a skillful physician, the nature of his disorder is such that confinement must be injurious, and may be fatal, we think he ought to be bailed."

If Justice Washington had no compunctions about applying rules of humanity to a man accused of piracy, and suffering only from a physical ailment, this court has ample precedent for admitting to bail Ezra Pound, who has been charged with a crime hardly more heinous than piracy, and not only appears to be insane at the present time, as a result of previous imprisonment, but may very likely be rendered permanently insane, and may lose his life, if imprisonment continues.

3

There was a brief recess while Mr. Matlack studied the documents and consulted with the Justice Department. He told the court that the government had no objection to a medical examination for Pound. The decision of Judge Laws follows:

"I have considered the motion filed in behalf of the defendant that he be admitted to bail or in the alternative that he be removed from his present place of imprisonment in the Washington Asylum and Jail to the custody of a hospital or other institution operated by the United States or the District of Columbia. From the showing made before me by counsel for the defendant, it appears advisable to have an examination and observation of the defendant made by physicians and that pending such an examination and report of their findings and pending the granting of opportunity to counsel for the prosecution to reply to the motion for bail, no action should be taken on such motion.

"Accordingly, the defendant is ordered remanded to the Washington Asylum and Jail with the recommendation that he be transferred to Gallinger Hospital or such other hospital as may be designated by authorized officials of the United States for examination and observation and for treatment, if found necessary. The motion for admission to bail is continued for further hearing until December 14, 1945; counsel for the United States will submit on or before December 10th any showing which they may desire to make in opposition to the said motion."

Pound was admitted to Gallinger Hospital on December 4, and was examined by four psychiatrists, three representing the government, the fourth the defendant. He was Dr. Wendell Muncie, of Baltimore, to whom Mr. Cornell had previously sent an account of his client, similar to the information contained in the affidavit, together with the *PM* article, a copy of Pound's April 23, 1942, broadcast, and a first draft of a portion of Canto LXXX, which afterward appeared in *The Pisan Cantos*. The broadcast will be found on p. 48; Canto LXXX deals with Pound's confinement in the DTC.

On December 14, following their examinations of Pound, the psychiatrists reported to Chief Judge Laws as follows:

FEDERAL SECURITY AGENCY
SAINT ELIZABETHS HOSPITAL
WASHINGTON 20, D.C.

December 14, 1945

Honorable Bolitha J. Laws,
Chief Justice, U.S. District Court,
Washington, D.C.

Sir:

The undersigned hereby respectfully report the results of their mental examination of Ezra Pound, now detained in Gallinger Hospital by transfer for observation from the District Jail on a charge of treason. Three of us (Drs. Gilbert, King, and Overholser) were appointed by your Honor to make this examination. At our suggestion, and with your approval, Dr. Wendell Muncie, acting upon the request of counsel for the accused, made an examination with us and associates himself with us in this joint report. Dr. Muncie spent several hours with the defendant, both alone and with us, on December 13, 1945, and the others of us have examined the defendant each on several occasions, separately and together, in the period from his admission to Gallinger Hospital on December 4, 1945 to December 13, 1945. We have had available to us the reports of laboratory, psychological and special physical examinations of the defendant and considerable material in the line of his writings and biographical data.

The defendant, now 60 years of age and in generally good physical condition, was a precocious student, specializing in literature. He has been a voluntary expatriate for nearly 40 years, living in England and France, and for the past 21 years in Italy, making an uncertain living by writing poetry and criticism. His poetry and literary criticism have achieved considerable recognition, but of recent years his preoccupation with monetary theories and economics has apparently obstructed his literary productivity. He has long been recognized as eccentric, querulous, and egocentric.

At the present time he exhibits extremely poor judgment as to his situation, its seriousness and the manner in which the charges are to be met. He insists that his broadcasts were not treasonable, but that all of his radio activities have stemmed from his self appointed mission to "save the Constitution." He is abnormally grandiose, is expansive and exuberant in manner, exhibiting pressure of speech, discursiveness, and distractibility. In our opinion, with advancing years his personality, for many years abnormal, has undergone further distortion to the extent that he is now suffering from a paranoid state which renders him mentally unfit to advise properly with counsel or to participate intelligently and reasonably in his own defense. He is, in other words, insane and mentally unfit for trial, and is in need of care in a mental hospital.

Respectfully submitted,

Joseph L. Gilbert, M.D.

Marion R. King, M.D.

Wendell Muncie, M.D.

Winfred Overholser, M.D.

The motion for bail was heard and denied on December 21. Pound was committed to St. Elizabeths Hospital, a government institution for the criminally insane, Dr. Winfred Overholser, superintendent. It appeared as though the case of the United States of America against him was over. But on January 16, 1946, the District Court heard and granted a motion by the Attorney General's office for a formal statutory inquisition into Pound's mental state.

This was held on February 13, 1946, before Judge Laws and a jury, Isaiah Matlack and Donald Anderson representing the Department of Justice, and Mr. Cornell the defendant. The names of the jurors were: Benjamin Abramson, William T. Berry, Thomas H. Broadus, Ethel M. Christie, Carroll K. Jenkins, Sr., Raymond M. Lawrenson, Frank A. Marceron, Edward T. Martowicz, Edward A. Mohler, Leonard W. Morris, Jesse W. Missear, and George E. Polen. Pound himself was not called to the stand, but spoke out once, during the cross-examination of Dr. Overholser.

nine

Morning Session:

Dr. Wendell Muncie

DISTRICT COURT OF THE UNITED STATES FOR THE
DISTRICT OF COLUMBIA

UNITED STATES OF AMERICA :
                            :
                            :

          against   : Criminal No. 76,028
                            :
                            :
                            :

EZRA POUND,   :
        Defendant :

Transcript of Testimony, Wednesday, February 13, 1946

Before: Hon. Bolitha J. Laws, Chief Justice of the District
Court of the United States for the District of Columbia
and a jury.

ISAIAH MATLACK, Esq. and DONALD ANDERSON, Esq. appearing on
behalf of the Department of Justice of the United States;

JULIEN CORNELL, Esq. appearing on behalf of the defendant.

THE CLERK OF THE COURT: The case of Ezra Pound.

THE COURT: Swear the jury.

THE CLERK OF THE COURT: The jurors will stand and raise your
right hands.

(Thereupon, the jurors were sworn on voir dire.)

THE COURT: Members of the jury, the case which the jury will be
impanelled to hear is one involving Ezra Pound, who is the defendant in a criminal case pending in this Court.

Mr. Pound is seated here. Will you stand, Mr. Pound, and face
the jury?

Thank you.

Certain representations have been made to the Court that Mr.
Pound is not in mental condition such as that he is able to participate with counsel in the trial of a criminal case, and is not in position to understand the full nature of the charges against him.

Based upon that showing which has been made to me by psychiatrists, I am going to impanel a jury to pass upon that question. In
the event the jury finds that his mental state is as has been represented to me, then Mr. Pound will not be brought to trial because,
under the law, it would not be proper to prosecute him if his
mental condition is as has been stated to me.

Now appearing for Mr. Pound is Mr. Julien Cornell of New
York. Will you stand, please?

Representing the United States Government in this case is Mr.
Matlack and Mr. Donald Anderson from the Department of Justice, who are now facing you.

Do any of you know Mr. Pound?

JUROR WINGFIELD: I do.

THE COURT: What is your name?

JUROR WINGFIELD: John Wingfield.

THE COURT: How long have you known him?

JUROR WINGFIELD: Ever since he has been there in the hospital.

THE COURT: Do you know some of the facts with reference to this matter?

JUROR WINGFIELD: Yes.

THE COURT: I will excuse you from this case.

Do any of the others know Mr. Pound?

Have any of you heard any of his broadcasts?

Do any of you know Mr. Cornell?

Do any of you know counsel for the United States, Mr. Matlack or Mr. Anderson?

Does any one of you know any reason why you cannot render a fair and impartial verdict in a matter of this type?

Has any member of your family, or any close friend, or have any of you been involved in any proceeding to attack their sanity?

Have you any further questions?

MR. MATLACK: We are satisfied.

MR. CORNELL: I would like Your Honor to ask the jury in view of the fact that this defendant broadcast statements during wartime in which he was highly critical of our Government, and also some statements which might be construed as anti-Semitic, whether they could render an impartial verdict?

THE COURT: Would any of you be prejudiced by reason of the fact that Mr. Pound made broadcasts that are said to have been against our Government, or against the Jewish race?

The question here is solely one of sanity of this particular individual, and under our law a man should not be brought to trial if he is in the condition they say he is, and it would be your duty to render a fair and impartial verdict in that case.

Is there any doubt in your mind about that?

THE COURT: Are you satisfied with the jury, Mr. Matlack?

MR. MATLACK: Yes, sir.

THE COURT: Mr. Cornell?

MR. CORNELL: I am satisfied.

THE COURT: Swear the jury.

(Thereupon, the above-named jury was sworn by the Clerk of the Court.)

MR. CORNELL: Call Dr. Muncie.

Thereupon Dr. WENDELL MUNCIE, a witness called on behalf of the Defendant, being the first duly sworn, was examined and testified as follows:

THE CLERK OF THE COURT: Be seated, please, and state your full name.

THE WITNESS: Dr. Wendell Muncie.

Direct Examination

BY MR. CORNELL.

Q. Dr. Muncie, will you state your profession?

A. I am a psychiatrist.

Q. Will you tell me what institutions you are connected with in your practice?

A. Johns Hopkins Hospital, Baltimore; Marine Hospital, Baltimore; Eaton Institute, Baltimore; and Mt. Alto. I am Associate Professor of Psychiatry at the Johns Hopkins Hospital, and consulting psychiatrist in other hospitals.

Q. How long have you been engaged in the practice of medicine and psychiatry?

A. In the practice of medicine since 1927, and in psychiatry since 1929.

Q. What hospital are you a graduate from?

A. Johns Hopkins.

Q. Have you written any books or papers on psychiatry?

A. A number of papers and a textbook.

Q. Is that book still used in the practice of psychiatry?

A. Well, it still sells.

Q. In the practice of your profession have you had occasion to engage in the examination of the sanity of people?

A. That is all I do, and treat them.

Q. On an average, how many persons whose sanity is in question do you see during a year?

A. I spend about 2200 hours either examining patients or treating patients in the course of a year, and in that time I suppose of those 2200 hours 500 of them represent new patients, maybe more.

Q. In the course of those investigations do you have occasion to investigate all types of mental disorders?

A. Yes, sir.

Q. Will you tell me, Dr. Muncie, when did you first examine the defendant here, Mr. Pound?

A. December 13, 1945.

Q. At that time he was already under indictment for this crime, as you have been informed, is that right?

A. Yes, sir.

Q. And where was he then confined?

A. He was in the Gallinger Hospital.

Q. Did you perform this examination in collaboration with any other physician?

A. Part of it was with the other three psychiatrists, but most of it I made myself.

Q. By the other three psychiatrists, do you mean those three doctors out there who are witnesses in this case?

A. Yes.

Q. Were you attempting to define his illness?

A. Yes.

Q. Will you state what symptoms you found in Mr. Pound?

A. Yes, sir. May I have reference to some notes?

Q. Certainly. Perhaps you had better turn to the jury so they can hear you clearly.

A. There are a number of things which attracted my attention in examining Mr. Pound, and these are essentially the items that appeared to me:

He has a number of rather fixed ideas which are either clearly delusional or verging on the delusional. One I might speak of, for instance, he believes he has been designated to save the Constitution of the United States for the people of the United States.

I will come back to this item in a minute.

Secondly, he has a feeling that he has the key to the peace of the world through the writings of Confucius, which he translated into

Italian and into English, and that if this book had been given proper circulation the Axis would not have been formed, we would be at peace now, and a great deal of trouble could have been avoided in the past, and this becomes his blueprint for world order in the future.

Third, he believes that with himself as a leader, a group of intellectuals could have gotten together in different countries, like Japan, for instance, where he is well thought of, to work for world order. He has a hatred of bureaucrats which goes back a long way, and one may conclude that his saving of the Constitution draws a clear distinction between the rights of the people and those who govern people.

He feels he was double-crossed in being brought back to this country, thinking that he was being brought back to aid the country because of his special connections in Italy, and that his double-cross was at the hands of the British Commandos.

So much for the rather fixed ideas he holds.

In addition to that, he shows a remarkable grandiosity. He feels that he has no peer in the intellectual field, although conceding that one or two persons he has assisted might, on occasion, do as good work as he did.

This grandiosity I speak of, in connection with the translation of Confucius, might have prevented the formation of the Axis, and that if he could only get to Japan and work through the poets over there he could work for world order, and if they could only get over here they could work for world order.

This all sounds as if it was clear-cut. Quite the contrary, it is not clear-cut, and the case from any psychiatric picture has a remarkable vagueness and when one attempts to follow his exposition of these vague ideas I, at least, have been left out on a limb every time. I would say he is unable to make a solution of his own fixed ideas, and he cannot explain or balance the significance of the difficulty in his thinking operations.

In addition to the vagueness, there is a considerable distractibility, as we call it, that is to say, he moves from topic to topic; for instance, if he is asked a specific question as to a specific situation he begins to make an answer and then all of a sudden is making a statement about a number of topics which may be clear in his mind but cannot be clear in the examiner's mind. There is a great push, and then a condition which we refer to as stupor when nothing comes. He just holds his head and nothing comes, and at those times he has complained of a feeling of emptiness in the forehead, or a feeling of pressure in the forehead also, and I did see an interesting phenomenon on one occasion:

The first time I saw him, December 13th, I referred in a social way to the fact that my brother had been a student at Wabash College, where he spent some six months in connection with his postgraduate career. He obviously did not remember my brother and the matter was passed off lightly. When I saw him on February 7th I was reintroduced to him by the other doctors, and his immediate comment was, "Yes, you have a brother," and "he was my best student, he had just come back from Europe, and he came from a family of the highest culture in Indiana."

Now, irrespective of the merits of this latter issue, this is pure confabulation, I would say it is a confusion of facts in the face of real lack of memory about my brother It is the only item I had that I could corroborate, although there may be other examples of confabulation. He complains of exhaustion as the cause of his breakdown in—

Q. Before you go on, Doctor, will you explain the cause of confabulation?

A. Confabulation may have a number of causes, with no ulterior motive, but ordinarily when we use the term, and I would think very strongly in that connection, it is occasioned by a definite loss of memory, and it usually appears in people with some kind of deteriorating process of the brain. I did not stress this point too much because it was just one item, and not necessary to my understanding of the case.

He believes the exhaustion is the cause of the breakdown in his thinking processes. His memory definitely is not keen. It takes time for the answer to come.

Now, in addition to these things which represent to my mind

the formal aspects of the disorder in the thinking process, vagueness, distractibility and confabulation, and the poor, not keen, memory, and things coming back very slowly, he definitely shows a very poor grasp of his present situation.

He felt, he tells me, that he was being brought back to this country to help the Government in understanding the Italian situation, and to work towards the rehabilitation of the world. He apparently did not realize that he was being brought back here for treason, and when he found that out his argument was that he must have been double-crossed and that it was, as I said, at the hands of the British Intelligence Service or Commandos.

That is how the patient appears to me, and it may not be necessary to go into further diagnosis.

Q. Doctor, I would like for you to go into a little more detail about his predicament, and how well he understands it.

A. He has two minds about that. At times he believes he could persuade any jury who could understand him of the fact that he had not committed treason. At other times, he states categorically that he is not of sound mind and could not participate effectively in his own defense. The latter I would concur with.

Q. Did you at any time ascertain whether he understood the nature of the offense?

A. Whether he understands the meaning of treason, or not, I do not know. He categorically denies that he committed anything like treason, in his mind, against the people of the United States.

Q. Were you able to discuss it with him sufficiently to find out whether or not he had any grasp of the nature of his alleged crime?

A. Such discussions, and there have been several, always end up in bringing in all the matters I talked about, the economic situation, Confucius, Japan, and so forth, but by no stretch of the imagination can you make him realize the seriousness of his predicament, and that is the astonishing thing, if you touch on his case and hospitalization, Confucius and these other things seemed to get roped in, and you end up with with a confusion of thoughts.

Q. In other words, he is not able to pursue a point logically, but he does confuse it with other ideas, is that right?

A. Yes.

Q. Were you able to discover whether any other mental difficulties had occurred in his previous life?

A. Well, all we know is from the record that he went through an unusual mental experience in a concentration camp in Italy, which, by all the records, must have been a profound emotional experience amounting, I suppose, to a panic state, but to suggest how it might be described technically, I don't know. But it was a rather severe emotional crisis he went through, at which time he was seen, I think, by some psychiatrists.

Q. Before that did you examine sufficient of his writings, and so on, to be able to determine whether or not this condition may have arisen in his earlier life?

A. I have read a great deal of his writings in connection with preparing this case, and it is my idea that there has been for a number of years a deterioration of the mental processes.

Q. Will you tell the jury what is your opinion as to Mr. Pound's ability to understand the meaning of a trial under this indictment for treason, and particularly his ability to consult with counsel and formulate a defense to the indictment?

A. I think he is not capable of doing any of those things.

Q. Would you think that your opinion would become more clear by giving it in medical diagnostic terminology, Dr. Muncie, or doesn't that add anything to the picture?

A. I don't think it does. Those are of a statistical nature. I would say in ordinary language he has been a peculiar individual for many, many years, and that on top of that in recent years, I don't know how long back, he has been engrossed with these things I have talked about as neurotic developments. For statistical purposes we could call this a paranoid condition.

Q. By "paranoid" do I understand that involves delusions and self-aggrandizement?

A. Yes.

Q. Do you know whether Mr. Pound in his present condition would be able to stand up under the rigors of a cross-examination?

A. That is predicting things into the future, and one cannot predict, but I think it would be rather dangerous to his welfare.

MR. MATLACK: If the Court please, I have no objection to the questions, but I do not think this should take into consideration what he might do in the future.

THE COURT: Well, if it was of today it would be all right.

If he were to go on trial at the present time, Doctor, do you think his nervous system would be able to sustain him throughout the trial?

THE WITNESS: I think it would be very doubtful, very hazardous.

MR. CORNELL: No more questions.

Cross-Examination

BY MR. MATLACK:

Q. How many times, Doctor, did you see Mr. Pound?

A. Twice. December 13th and February 7th.

Q. How long a period did you talk to him?

A. The first time between three and four hours, the second time two hours.

Q. During the time you saw Mr. Pound December 13th, which you say was a period of three hours—

A. Practically, yes.

Q. How much of that time did you talk to him alone?

A. Most of the time, all but about 15 minutes.

Q. And the rest of the time by yourself after introduction by the other doctors?

A. Yes.

Q. Did you go into his history when you went to interview him?

A. I had a statement from Mr. Cornell of Mr. Pound's situation up to the date of his being taken prisoner in Italy and being brought back here.

Q. Did you have any history back of that?

A. I had excerpts from newspapers, and from people who are in better position to judge his literary ability.

Q. By newspaper articles you refer to those contained in the petition filed here?

A. Yes.

Q. Did you have any other history given to you by Mr. Pound as to his condition?

A. No, sir.

Q. Did you have any information furnished to you by Mr. Pound as to where he was born, for instance?

A. Oh, I had secondary information to which I had access, hospital records at Gallinger, which was rather complete.

Q. Did you consider his past life from the time he left the United States?

A. At considerable length.

Q. Was he able to discuss that intelligently with you?

A. Well, he gave me some of the facts.

Q. And did he give them to you correctly as the hospital record showed?

A. I think so.

Q. Did he have any loss of memory as to his past history?

A. He said that there was a period of three to four years preceding the Italian capture, not capture, but since he gave himself up to the American Army, that he is not sure about the allocation of events in time. I have no way of corroborating that. That may or may not be true.

Q. Is he able to correlate events in the last four or five years in all ordinary particulars?

A. It would depend on the events, I think.

Q. Do you know what events he was referring to?

A. No, it was nothing that I could check up on so I did not pursue it any further.

Q. What bearing did Pound's history, as given to you by him have upon your diagnosis?

A. It has this bearing, that I think it gives indisputable proof of a peculiar personality for many years. That is the basis for my diagnosis of the paranoid make-up.

Q. Let me ask you this: Do you think a peculiar personality denotes insanity?

A. No, not in the strict sense of the term.

Q. Do you think that the peculiar personality that you say he has—I presume that is your impression from talking to him— prevents him from properly understanding the charge that he has been charged with and prevents him from discussing the matter with his counsel?

A. That doesn't, but that is not all of the diagnosis. That is the background diagnosis. The present situation is something else, as I have indicated.

Q. Now, what was the nature of the examination you gave Mr. Pound during the time you saw him?

A. A psychiatric examination. It is a recital and examination of material that you can check on today, I would say, by direct examination, having to do with his mental content, or his thought, his type of thinking process and his intellectual capacity.

Q. I think it might be of help to the jury, I know it would be to me, if you would tell us a little more in detail what a psychiatric examination consists of.

A. There are two aspects; you give the patient a chance to state spontaneously anything he wants to state which he thinks relevant to his complaint, spontaneously going to great lengths and bringing in a great deal of material which may or may not be relevant to the present situation. After you have satisfied yourself about his understanding of the situation, and the material he would like to produce about it, then you begin to ask specific questions to satisfy yourself on those things, whether his mentality is out of order, and his intellectual resources are out of order, or whether his thinking processes are out of order.

Those questions have to do with material that you can check on, current events, retention of thought, and so forth.

Q. How did you find his memory?

A. His memory, as far as I could find was all right, except for a substantial period in the concentration camp where there appears to have been a blackout of memory.

Q. That would not be unusual, in your opinion, Doctor, under such stress or strain?

A. It is unusual when related to the emotional panic which he experienced there at that concentration camp, and to which concentration he was not used to.

Q. Don't you think it is rather normal for a person subsequently arrested for a charge of treason to be under great emotional stress?

A. I wouldn't know, Mr. Matlack. One might suppose that would be an incentive to keep your thoughts about you. The answer is, I don't know.

Q. Have you had occasion to examine many cases of people who are under criminal charges?

A. Not many. I have had occasion to but I haven't done it.

Q. So you don't know whether being under a criminal charge causes emotional stress?

A. I know they write books on that topic.

Q. Did you give any consideration to the writings and publications of Mr. Pound in coming to your conclusions?

A. Not as to his broadcast subjects. A man has to try to understand the background of his personality. I think one would have to.

Q. Has the nature of the charge, namely, that of treason, had anything to do with it, in your opinion?

A. No, sir.

Q. In other words, what I have in mind is that if the charge had been something less than treason, say embezzlement, something of that sort, which did not relate to his writings and broadcasts, would your opinion be that his mental condition would be different than you found it to be?

A. No, that has nothing to do with it.

Q. You do not think that the charge itself relating to writing, or his broadcasts which is, of course, in his line of endeavor, namely, writing, would have any bearing?

A. As far as I am able to judge in the case, I would say no.

Q. Now, you said he had fixed ideas, if I understood you correctly, and the first one was that he thought he had an assigned task to save the Constitution. Do you think that in itself indicates any inability to consult with counsel and to understand the charge he is charged with?

A. No.

Q. There are a lot of people, aren't there, with certain fixed ideas that we, as laymen, may think are peculiar, which do not in themselves indicate insanity?

A. Yes.

Q. And your second statement, correct me if I am wrong, is that he believes he has the key to the peace of the world through the translations of Confucius, and that if the world had listened to him in that respect there would not have been any formation of the Axis?

A. Yes.

Q. Would that in itself make you say that he was insane?

A. No.

Q. And then I think you said the third thing was that he felt, with himself as leader, if a group of intellectuals could have gotten together with certain poets, or other people, in Japan and possibly elsewhere, that they could have arrived at a solution of some kind of peace, but that they did not do it?

A. Yes.

Q. Does that indicate insanity?

A. It indicates to my mind that he is getting farther and farther away from the reality of the situation. Whether that in itself constitutes insanity I would say no, one is entitled to some queer ideas without being called insane.

Q. And then I think you said he had a hatred of bureaucrats. I think a lot of people have that, don't they?

A. Yes.

Q. And that, in itself, would not necessarily indicate that he was insane?

A. That's right.

Q. And the fifth fixed idea, as I take it, is that he feels he was double-crossed in being brought back to this country, that he thought he was being brought back to consult about Italy but found he was charged with treason?

A. Yes.

Q. Did you talk to him about this charge of treason at all?

A. Yes.

Q. Did he tell you that he had been indicted in 1943 as a result of his broadcasts?

A. No, that came to him as a surprise later on.

Q. But he did know it before he was brought back to this country?

A. I think he did.

Q. And did he know that he was placed in a concentration camp because of those charges?

A. No, he said he turned himself in to the American forces voluntarily because of his knowledge concerning Italy.

Q. And that was his explanation, I mean he did not vary from that at all?

A. No, that was his explanation.

Q. When did he say he learned that he was charged with treason?

A. I really don't know that.

Q. At the time you examined him in December, did you think that there was any question in his mind that he was charged with treason?

A. Oh, no, he knew it then.

Q. Do you think he understood what treason was?

A. Well, I think he does.

Q. Do you think he understands the nature of the charge, and that possibly he would be tried for the crime of treason?

A. Yes.

Q. Now, what do you mean, Doctor, when you say he shows grandiosity? What does that mean?

A. It means an exaggerated opinion of one's self.

Q. Is that a sign of insanity?

A. If it gets out of bounds it is.

Q. When does it get out of bounds, in your opinion?

A. It gets out of bounds in certain paranoid states, and in certain minor conditions which I do not think enter into the picture.

BY THE COURT:

Q. That is very common to paranoia, isn't it?

A. Yes.

BY MR. MATLACK:

Q. What is paranoia?

A. Paranoia is a mental state in which there is a fixed state of delusion with logical inferences resting on an untenable hypothesis. If one grants as reasonable the hypothesis, then all the rest of the system of ideas must be true. Pure paranoia is rare. There is logical thinking, and you cannot therefore refute his ideas if you admit his original premise.

The finding here is that all ideas are fixed in the sense that he comes back to them all the time, but none of them is clear. It is all vague. That is the essential difference.

Q. You mean vague to the examiner?

A. Yes, of course.

Q. Are they all based on a general subject, one subject, we will say?

A. There are a number of ramifications and, as I say, if you touch on one of these you always bring in this one. If one might use an analogy, if you touch an octopus on one tentacle all the others react. That shows that there is systematization of the material and that it is vague.

Q. Now, you spoke about him having some difficulty in his thinking operations. Just what difficulty did you find?

A. I testified it was vague, that is to say, he is unable to present a logical statement about any aspect of his case in his present situation, and, secondly his distractibility. I forgot to add that this distractibility is the result of internal things, not external things.

For example, if you and I were talking on some topic and somebody came in and yelled something, the noise of it might distract us from our present topic; that would be an outer distractibility, but his comes from within, and he has to be forcibly brought back to the topic at hand.

Q. Does this distractibility underlie this one idea of the theory of economics he has?

A. That is mixed up in it. Its ramifications are such that I do not understand it, although I have tried to.

Q. Do you think his theories and ideas are superior to the average man's intelligence on the subject that he is talking about?

A. I think he thinks they are, but there did not seem any way of proving it.

Q. What would be the norm on that?

A. I don't know that one could conceive what is the norm on it; I can only say that I could not follow his argument on numerous occasions. Whether I believe in it or not has nothing to do with it. I couldn't follow it.

Q. Now, you say that you examined him again on February 6th or 7th.

A. February 7th.

Q. Did you examine him alone or with others?

A. With three other psychiatrists.

Q. You had the three with you at that time. What did that examination consist of?

A. About the same thing.

Q. And that took about two hours?

A. About two hours less the facts of the history because that was well-established.

Q. Do you think that there was any possibility during the two hours that you were talking with him that he might have been feigning in any way?

A. Oh, no, I don't think so.

Q. You don't think that would have been possible?

A. No, he was most cooperative.

Q. Was the examination on February 7th any different from the one on December 13th?

A. Only as I said, I spent less time on the actual historical material with which we were acquainted at that time. It had to do with his present situation essentially.

Q. You think that Mr. Pound has delusions, did I understand you to say?

A. Yes.

Q. And that has to do with self-importance?

A. Yes.

Q. Any other delusions?

A. I think he approaches quite clearly the delusional; he approaches the delusional in his vague schemes for the rehabilitation of the world. Most of us would be appalled by that task, but it does not seem to faze Mr. Pound.

Q. Do you think it is a delusion any different than some of these other European leaders had in that they had an idea they were going to conquer the world?

A. I haven't had a chance to examine them.

Q. But what I am getting at is whether you think it might be similar?

A. It might be, but I have never examined them.

Q. In connection with the charge of treason, did Mr. Pound discuss with you his activities in broadcasting?

A. Yes, he told us about his broadcasts.

Q. And what did he say about that with respect to whether he thought that it was treason, or not?

A. He said that it was not treason.

Q. Now, did the fact that he did not consider it treason have any bearing on the judgment which you found in this connection?

A. It would have this importance: it shows clearly that he was out of touch with a very large segment of the world, and it shows more clearly than anything else perhaps how his world was built for himself. You and I are living in what one is pleased to call the realities of the situation.

Q. Might it not be that he believed that he was not exactly legally liable for treason?

A. If you will leave the word "legal" out I will agree with you.

Q. Wouldn't that be a matter which indicated that he was not of sound mind?

A. Yes.

Q. Now, I think you answered the question that he understands, in your opinion, the charge he was under?

A. Yes.

Q. And that he understood that he was brought over here to be tried for that charge?

A. Yes.

Q. Now, will you explain to the jury why you do not think he is able to consult with counsel?

A. Because I do not have any doubt but that his counsel would have the same experience I had with him, namely, that when he would try to pin him down to anything he would be left out on a limb just as I was time after time through his distractibility and vagueness.

Q. Do you think he does not realize he made these broadcasts?

A. Oh, yes, he knows that.

Q. And that he did write the scripts from which he broadcast?

A. I didn't ask him if he wrote them, but I presume he did.

Q. And did he tell you that he had turned over to the Government the manuscripts and scripts?

A. He did not tell me.

Q. Did you ask him how many times, or how often he broadcast?

A. That is a matter of record. I had the record on that.

Q. You did not think that that entered into the situation of whether he was able to consult with counsel?

A. No.

Q. And in your opinion, as I understand it, the reason that it would be hard to confer with counsel is that it is hard to stay on a subject, is that right?

A. It is hard to stay on a subject, and when you end up you don't finish with any coherent statement or intelligent thought.

Q. Well, he answered your questions?

A. No, no, when I say, "Mr. Pound, you are out to defend the Constitution; now, that is a lengthy document, will you tell me what items are you out to defend specifically?", why, he will say, "The President is a magistrate with delegated powers." That is all I could get on this question.

From then on he goes through all those ramifications about Confucius, and Heaven knows what.

Q. Doesn't he discuss the money and other clauses in the Constitution?

A. Yes.

Q. And that would be reasonable evidence he knew how he is going to save the Constitution?

A. By inference, but there isn't any clear statement, and then he goes on to these other things I have indicated which may play a part in the general scheme of things to him, but not to me.

Q. What do you think about his intelligence?

A. That was investigated at length by the psychiatrists at the hospital. I do not remember the figure, but I think it is superior.

Q. You think he is superior in intelligence?

A. Yes.

MR. CORNELL: Your Honor, I object to that. The other doctor is here, and to have this doctor testify would be hearsay.

BY MR. MATLACK:

Q. What is your observation of his intelligence?

A. I think it is not too high at the present time because of actual difficulties in his thinking processes.

Q. His memory, you say, is good though?

A. Except for the period of the last summer, as far as I can make out.

MR. MATLACK: I think that is all, Doctor. Thank you, very much.

MR. CORNELL: May I ask a few more questions, if your Honor please, in rebuttal?

THE COURT: All right.

Redirect Examination

BY MR. CORNELL:

Q. Doctor, Mr. Matlack questioned you about the length of that examination and about the investigations which you had made into Mr. Pound's history. I suppose you also had the record of the period he was under observation in the hospital, is that right?

A. Yes.

Q. How long a period was that?

A. I think it was around ten days in Gallinger Hospital.

Q. That was the first time, and what was the other?

A. He has been in St. Elizabeths about two months.

Q. And all that time he was under psychiatric observation?

A. Yes.

Q. So that you had the benefit not only of your examination but of the information gained by the other doctors in those two months?

A. Yes.

Q. Now, the Assistant Attorney General has questioned you somewhat concerning the effect of Mr. Pound's being a writer and also the fact that this is a treason indictment, and I am going to ask you a hypothetical question:

Assuming that you knew nothing whatever about Mr. Pound

being a poet, a man of some literary attainments, and assume that you knew nothing about his broadcasts over the Italian radio, and being charged with treason, and that he came in off the street and you questioned him as you did, would you, without knowing these special facts, be of the same opinion as to his ability to meet a charge against him?

A. Yes, I would.

Q. In other words, then, it is not based on anything extraordinary you found about Mr. Pound?

A. No.

Q. But his difficulty to follow through a certain chain of reasoning?

A. Yes.

Q. Even assuming that you would not be able to put his mental illness in any particular classification, would you say that his inability to reason, and his distractibility would prevent a lawyer from adequately defending him?

A. Yes, I would say that is the vital thing here. What we call it is for the purpose of our diagnosis.

Q. Now, Mr. Matlack questioned you about those delusions Mr. Pound has. I suppose you, or I, or others could have some one of them and it would not have any significance, but it is the accumulation of delusions along different lines which leads you to suspect a deranged condition here?

A. Yes.

Q. You mentioned the word "systematization." Do you mean by that that he has a system of reasoning which is embedded in his mentality so that it is impossible for him to think outside of that system?

A. Yes.

Q. Would it make it impossible for him to understand this charge made against him?

A. I think it would be very difficult. I will go further and say impossible.

Q. I am not sure that this is a proper question, but do you think it would add anything to your description of him if we were to put him on the witness stand and question him concerning this case and see how he reacts?

A. Well, I can only say I feel sure enough in my own mind that my opinion would be corroborated by everybody hearing him.

Q. Do you think you have been able to describe his present mental reactions so that it is not necessary to distress him by putting him on the stand?

A. I would think so.

MR. CORNELL: That is all.

Recross-Examination

BY MR. MATLACK:

Q. Do I understand you now to say that you base your opinion partly on some hospital records from the time you first examined him up to February 7th?

A. Yes, sir.

Q. How much of your opinion is based on that?

A. Nothing essential because they found the same things we did. It is a static picture so far as memory is concerned, and nothing startling was added. That is, what I term confabulation came out graphically in connection with his inability to think. He was grandiose and hard to talk to, and this second time he had more of that than when I saw him the first time.

MR. MATLACK: That is all, Doctor.

BY THE COURT:

Q. Let me ask you a question, Doctor. You made a written report to me in conjunction with other psychiatrists under date of December 14th, did you not?

A. Yes.

Q. Now, did each of the psychiatrists examine him separately, or did you have your examination together?

A. No, all but about fifteen minutes was my own examination.

Q. I do not think it was brought out that your examination was in connection with Dr. Overholser of St. Elizabeths?

A. Yes.

Q. And Dr. King of the Public Health Service?

A. Yes.

Q. And Dr. Gilbert of Gallinger?

A. Yes.

Q. And all four of you joined in that report to me and reached the same conclusion?

A. Yes.

Q. And that was the same conclusion you arrived at?

A. Yes, it was the same thing.

Q. There has been no disagreement at all?

A. No.

THE COURT: That is all.

(Witness excused.)

ten

Morning Session:

Dr. Marion R. King

MR. CORNELL: Call Dr. King.

Thereupon—

DR. MARION R. KING

was called as a witness for and on behalf of the Defendant, and being first duly sworn, was examined and testified as follows:

THE CLERK OF THE COURT: Be seated, please, and state your full name.

THE WITNESS: My name is Marion R. King.

Direct Examination

BY MR. CORNELL:

Q. Dr. King, will you kindly state your official capacity at the present time?

A. I am Medical Director of the United States Public Health Service, also of the Bureau of Prisons of the Department of Justice.

Q. Then you are the chief medical officer having to do with criminal matters insofar as the Government is concerned?

A. Insofar as health, mental and physical health of prisoners of the Bureau of Prisons is concerned, yes, sir.

Q. Are you in charge of medical matters relating to all Federal prisoners?

A. Yes, sir.

Q. How long have you held that position?

A. Since September 1, 1922.

If you please, I would like to supplement that, that my connection with the Bureau of Prisons is in an advisory capacity. I do not have complete charge of all matters of health or otherwise. It is under the supervision and direction of the Director of Prisons.

Q. Then what is your connection in the Public Health Service?

A. In the office of Public Health Service of the Bureau of Prisons in charge of medical and psychiatric care of prisoners.

Q. Then you are associated with the Bureau of Prisons?

A. Yes, my title is Medical Director.

Q. Medical Director of the Bureau of Prisons?

A. Yes, and also of the Public Health Service.

Q. How long have you been with the Public Health Service?

A. 26 years.

Q. Were you in private practice prior to that time?

A. I was in the Medical Corps of the Army during the first war, First World War, and then in private practice for approximately 18 months, and then entered the Public Health Service.

Q. During your connection with the Public Health Service have you specialized in psychiatry?

A. A great deal of it.

Q. Approximately at the present time how much of your time is taken up with psychiatric matters?

A. Approximately 50 per cent.

Q. Where did you go to medical school?

A. Stanford University.

Q. Did you have any postgraduate training?

A. Yes.

Q. Are you the author of any works on psychiatric problems?

A. Some articles dealing with mental health of the prisoners. I was instrumental in the development of physicians' treatment and study of borderline mental cases at Springfield, Missouri.

Q. Do you regard yourself as having special knowledge in the psychiatric field?

A. Yes.

Q. Will you tell us on what occasions you have examined Mr. Pound, and what other investigations concerning him you have made?

A. I examined the defendant on at least four occasions at Gallinger Hospital during December, 1945. Subsequently I examined him on one occasion alone at St. Elizabeths Hospital. That was January 29, 1946. And then jointly with three other physicians on February 7, 1946 I examined him.

Q. Those other physicians are Drs. Muncie, Overholser, and Gilbert?

A. Yes.

Q. The other three doctors who are here this morning, is that right?

A. That is right.

Q. Did you also make any investigation of his previous life as revealed in his writings, for instance, or his own accounts of his earlier days?

A. Yes, careful consideration was given to his life-long history, including his achievements and progress, and contact and dealings with others.

Q. How much have you read of his literary output?

A. Very little of the poetry. I have seen one of the cantos, and samples of poetry that have been reproduced from others.

Q. Have you read any of his economic tracts?

A. Yes.

Q. And have you read the text of any of the broadcasts which it is said he made from Italy?

A. Yes.

Q. Have you also had the benefit of records of psychiatric observation at Gallinger and St. Elizabeths Hospital?

A. Yes, sir.

Q. How long a period did those records cover?

A. From December 4, 1945.

Q. And to when did they run?

A. To the date of the last examination.

Q. Now, from your examination of him, and investigation of records of observation in the hospitals, are you able to give an opinion as to whether Mr. Pound is possessed of sufficient mental capacity to understand and intelligently participate in the defense of the indictment here which charges him with treason?

A. Yes.

Q. Can you give us your opinion, and also the reasoning on which it is based?

A. After rather careful consideration of his life-long history, and especially his progress during the last few years, it is my opinion that he has always been a sensitive, eccentric, cynical person, and these characteristics have been accentuated in the last few years to such an extent that he is afflicted with a paranoid state of psychotic proportions which renders him unfit for trial.

Q. I presume a person can be psychotic, might even have paranoid tendencies, and be eccentric and cynical, and still be able to stand trial, is that true?

A. Yes.

Q. What other considerations are there in his case which make him unable to stand trial, in your opinion?

A. He has deviated from his chosen profession in that he has become preoccupied with economic and governmental problems to such an extent that during discussion of those problems he manifests such a sudden and such a marked feeling and tone that he reaches the point of exhaustion, and this unusual propensity, intense feeling, is quite characteristic of paranoid conditions and is sufficient, in my opinion, to permit, at least create, considerable confusion; at least that was the situation when I examined him, so that it is very difficult for him to explain his theories and proposals in a clear and concise logical manner.

He also exhibited considerable distractibility, easily distracted from the subject of the conversation, and it was difficult for him to come back to the point under discussion.

Q. Have you seen such symptoms as those in other men under accusation of crime, or men convicted of crime?

A. I have seen many cases of this type not only among people who were charged with crime, or convicted of crime, but also among those who have not been charged with an offense.

Q. Do you regard this inability to reason properly, this condition of distractibility, as the major reason why it would be, in your opinion, impossible for him to stand trial?

A. One of the major reasons.

Q. Did you discuss the actual nature of his case sufficiently to determine whether he is able to reason intelligently about it?

A. Yes.

Q. And is he able to reason about it intelligently?

A. No, not in a logical manner over a long period of time.

Q. In other words, he may be able to reason for a time, and then exhaustion and intense emotional disturbance would distract so that he cannot continue indefinitely, is that right?

A. That is correct.

Q. Would you tell us who it was that asked you to make this examination in the first place?

A. The Director of the Bureau of Prisons.

Q. That is Mr. Bennett?

A. Yes.

Q. And do you know at whose instance Mr. Bennett asked you to make this examination?

A. The Chief Justice of the District Court of the District of Columbia.

Q. That is Mr. Chief Justice Laws who is presiding here?

A. Yes, sir.

Q. And I made no request of you as defense counsel to intervene in the case, did I?

A. No.

Q. So that it was at a request coming from the Chief Justice of the District Court of the District of Columbia that you examined Mr. Pound?

A. The request was made to Mr. Bennett and passed on.

Q. And previous to your first examination of Mr. Pound did you have any discussions with me about his case?

A. No.

Q. I am going to ask you a question which I put to Dr. Muncie: Assume that Mr. Pound was not the unusual person that he is, and that he had not been charged with having committed the extraordinary crime he is charged with; assume that he was just another person under a charge for some petty offense, just a man in the street, would you have any different opinion about him in regard to his ability to undergo a criminal trial?

A. In evaluating the mental condition of any defendant one must always consider culture, intelligence and other traits. I think that in this particular case, the superior intelligence, the choice of professional field and the favorable progress in that particular activity are important factors, because the deviation from that field, the constant preoccupation with other activities, are significant in this case.

Q. You spoke of personal history of the individual.

A. This particular individual, yes.

Q. Then the fact that he is a great literary figure, and the fact that he is supposed to have committed treason, wouldn't enter into it?

A. No.

Q. This emotion, exhaustion and inability to reason, would that make it difficult or impossible for Mr. Pound to go through the ordeal of a trial?

A. Yes.

Q. If at the start he had some semblance of reason, do you think he would be able to keep that balance throughout the trial?

A. I don't think he would, judging from my experience with him. In my observations during the examinations he became exhausted and intensely wrought up when discussing these problems which have a bearing on his case, to such an extent that on two or three occasions he almost reached the point of collapse, and I am quite convinced that that would be repeated under certain conditions, and I am sure a trial would involve that.

Q. If trial would subject him to the state you speak about, do you think that would bring on collapse?

A. Yes.

Q. Do you mean physical or mental or both?

A. Both. The physical would be induced by the intense emotional tension.

Q. Just one more question; you mentioned distractibility. Would you try to explain to the jury in what way his reasoning could be said to be distractible? What have you found in him that causes you to use that term?

A. I found it was difficult for him to pursue a topic of conversation in a logical, reasonable and persistent manner. He gets sidetracked and talks about some other subject, possibly closely allied but not definitely connected.

Q. Was there any tendency when he got sidetracked to go off on the same track again?

A. Yes.

Q. What does he usually get into?

A. Usually the trend involves economic theories and proposals and much of it revolved about his revision of the monetary system.

Q. Then if you undertook to question him about his activities in Rome he would get off into this sidetrack on monetary theories?

A. Yes.

MR. CORNELL: That is all.

Cross-Examination

BY MR. ANDERSON:

Q. Doctor, if he got off on this sidetrack on a question could you get him to answer it again later?

A. Yes.

Q. Could you get him to repeat it again when he would get sidetracked?

A. Sometimes.

Q. Did you ask him about his life history?

A. Yes.

Q. And did he tell you about his life history correctly as far as you could tell from the other records that you had?

A. Yes.

Q. Did you ask him about his activities in Italy?

A. Yes.

Q. During the course of the examination?

A. Yes.

Q. And what did he tell you about those?

A. He went to Italy about 1924. His health was not too good at that time. He submitted to two or three operations. I do not remember whether they were all carried out in Paris or whether it was finished in Italy, but he had been in Italy on those occasions.

He had studied the Romance languages, and was very much interested in Italian culture, and after that Italy was his principal headquarters.

He resided there, and as far as his own ability was concerned he did a lot of work in translating and investigating Oriental classics, and during that period, too, he was very much concerned with political, economic and monetary problems. He became preoccupied with such matters to such an extent that it interfered largely with his own profession, without any profit or gain incidentally. One point I think is significant, that he became so consumed with these other fields because he developed a belief that most government officials were tyrannical and it behooved him to do what he could to overcome that and safeguard the citizens' rights. Therefore, he wrote two pamphlets on economics and became very greatly concerned and interested in such matters.

As time went on his enthusiasm became greater, and there is no question but that he has a lot of sudden, emotional feeling in connection with these hobbies, or these special interests, so that during the time of examinations he constantly told me about these ideas and beliefs with all the energy of which he was capable, which indicated that these matters more or less dominated his life, dominated his feelings.

He was inclined to argue and discuss them almost to the point of exhaustion. That is all indicative of a paranoid condition. That is really the evidence, as I interpret the case, the evidence of mental illness. It is not a case of well balanced, well developed resentment, people usually have some hostility when their feelings are hurt or they imagine they have been discriminated against. Something of that kind occurs to average individuals almost every day. But here we have a case where something happened many years ago. For example, he told a story of being mistreated or abused by a minor consular official in Paris in 1940, and elaborated on that as an example of the tyranny of government officials. It may be very true that he was mistreated, but that is not sufficient justification for such a reaction.

As for the life and vocation in which he was proficient, his work was outstanding, but he became sidetracked, and thereafter appointed himself as guardian of the citizenry to abolish enmities of an international type.

Q. Did he tell you about his writing of manuscripts and making broadcasts during the war?

A. Yes, sir.

Q. And from what he had told you did his answers and comments seem logical?

A. No.

Q. And in what respect?

A. His statements in that respect were usually vague, sometimes almost incoherent. It was difficult to ascertain his true motives because it was difficult for him to explain it and, incidentally, that was one of his worries, to have people understand him. He has a belief that he is misunderstood.

He implies that all his efforts, including his trip to the United States in 1939, and later his broadcasts, were carried out for the purpose of putting over these ideas and theories which he felt would bring about peace and order.

Now, another point I think is of significance here is this. I am convinced he glorifies in his rebelliousness rather than disguising it, and that again is indicative of a paranoid condition or paranoid state.

I think it is true, however, that some of his utterances, and maybe some of his output, is willful, that it should be regarded as willful, deliberate, and it might be classified as normal but, as I have indicated, I think much of it is indicative of a mental abnormality.

I think I should say it is impossible to sift out the absolute normal from the significant abnormal findings and facts, and in my judgment the latter predominate; that is to say, this paranoid state which now, to my mind, has been present for many, many years, has increased to such an extent that it has influenced his entire life, and through his own folly, and due to this defect, he has got himself into trouble more than once.

It is also significant, I think, that he has never hesitated, not only in these matters we are just talking about, but also problems that have been incident to his own person and profit, he has never hesitated to criticize, or vilify, or condemn others in no uncertain terms, even without provocation, and without good cause, or without any cause. Without question he has been his own worst enemy in that respect.

Q. By profession he is a poet, isn't he?

A. That's right, that is what I refer to.

Q. Have you read his poetry?

A. Some of it.

Q. And have you read poetry by other poets?

A. Some.

Q. And would the fact, if it is a fact, that you had some difficulty in understanding his poetry, would that have an effect in reaching your conclusion that poetry was not important to him, meaning the defendant?

A. It is my conviction from what I have heard from others who are qualified in the field of poetry, which incidentally I am not, that his achievements have been outstanding in that particular field, and he has been very successful in that particular field.

Q. Do you know how old he is at the present time?

A. He is 60 years old.

Q. Would his age have anything to do with his condition, in your opinion?

A. No.

Q. I believe you stated you had examined him four times in 1945 and once in January, and once in February?

A. That's right.

Q. Would you tell us briefly what type of examination you made at that time?

A. I examined him alone for at least two hours duration, and attempted to follow a plan which is standard in conducting psychiatric examination, and I found, after starting the examination, that I would have more information about the patient by permitting him to go ahead and talk. He chafes under cross-examination and restrictions, but does pretty well when allowed to proceed on his own accord; it is his own statement that he can explain his feelings and his ideas very much better if he is allowed to let the subject flow and not be interrupted too much.

Q. So the examinations were rather informal in that respect?

A. As a matter of fact, he was permitted to recline on a bed when I examined him alone. That again was helpful in gaining me his cooperation because for a long period of time he had been accustomed to doing a lot of his work while reclining in bed, but in the joint examination with the others it was conducted in rather a formal manner in a room sitting in chairs.

Q. Did you make a physical examination?

A. I did not personally, no.

Q. Was one made in your presence?

A. No, sir.

Q. Do you know who made one?

A. A physician at Gallinger Hospital, and I also understood at St. Elizabeths.

Q. In making your examination did you consider his life history, and the examination made at the hospital?

A. Yes.

Q. Have you seen the report of the examination at the hospital, or know what it was?

A. Yes.

Q. What was that?

A. There was no serious condition, or serious disease or significant physical abnormality; nothing found that would affect his mental condition.

Q. Or his ability to stand trial?

A. No.

Q. Would the fact that Mr. Pound is charged with treason in this case, would that have any greater bearing on his mental condition, more than if he was charged with any other crime?

A. No.

Q. What classification would you state for Mr. Pound's mental condition according to your classifications pertaining to mental illness?

A. I would say that would fall in the category of paranoid states, sometimes called paranoid conditions. That is not a very satisfactory term because it is part way between so-called paranoid schizophrenia or dementia praecox, paranoid type, and true paranoia. There are all types of gradations between the extremes, and it is my opinion that he falls in between those two extremes.

Q. Does he have a split personality?

A. No.

Q. Just what is it that makes you place him in that category?

A. He does not have the clear, well-defined systematized delusions of the paranoiac type; neither does he have the disassociation, the personal hallucinations or delusions, the disordered delusions that go with the dementia praecox, paranoid type, at the other extreme, but he does have a rather diffuse paranoid reaction which falls somewhere between those two fields, and that is the reason I would not classify him as a dementia praecox patient, or a case of true paranoia.

Q. In your opinion does he understand that he is charged with treason in this court? Does he know that that is what he is charged with?

A. Yes, sir.

Q. And does he know the effect that that may have on him, that he must stand trial and may be acquitted or convicted?

A. Yes, I think he understands that.

Q. Is he able to advise his attorney relative to the facts, the cause, and what he did?

A. No, not in a reasonable manner.

Q. What do you mean by a reasonable manner?

A. I mean that he is so distractible, and has such a pressure of speech, and he becomes so excited that it is impossible to talk with him over a long period of time, or consult with him in a logical manner without him becoming completely exhausted.

Q. Well, if the attorney would take the lead, and if he could be able to divert his mind, do you think he would be able to aid in his defense?

A. I don't think so. Judging from my conversations with him, he was unable to give you a clear view at all of his defense or his motives, his actions, or his operations in connection with his past activities.

Q. Does the fact that Mr. Pound might think that what he did was not treasonable have an effect in arriving at your opinion here?

A. To a minor extent. I think he is devoid of the niceties of a true understanding of his condition. He does not believe he is a mentally sick person. He does not believe that he is guilty of a serious offense against the United States.

He believes that he is so superior, and so important, and has such information that he should be used as an agent of the United States.

He believes that he could be useful to this country if he were designated as a diplomat, or agent, and sent to Japan, for instance, or even to Russia, to deal with the people over there, with the idea now of maintaining the peace of the world, and then prior to the war he thinks he could have prevented the war because of this special information he claims to have.

Q. That could be a difference of opinion, could it not, Doctor?

A. Yes; of course, that is my opinion.

Q. However, the fact that we differ would not affect his sanity or insanity, would it?

A. I don't think a sane man in his status would make such a proposal.

Q. Do you think he is feigning insanity, in any way?

A. No.

Q. How much consideration did you give to his writings in arriving at your determination?

A. To the extent that his writings on the monetary system, as far as I can ascertain, carried very little weight in this country, or elsewhere, although he had devoted a good deal of time to them. Over a period of many years he persisted in devoting too much time to matters of this type.

Q. Did you also consider his poetry in arriving at your conclusion?

A. Yes.

Q. What consideration did you give to that?

A. I concluded he was a very great poet because I read some of the opinions of experts in that field. That is not based on my particular evaluation of poetry because, as I indicated before, I am not qualified in that field.

Q. Are you qualified in the diplomatic field and economic field?

A. No.

Q. And did what poetry you did read of his make good sense?

A. I think what I read was all right.

Q. The fact that he may have had grandiose ideas, and a good idea of himself, is not peculiar particularly?

A. Not as to being a poet.

Q. And he is one of the leading poets of today?

A. Yes.

Q. And not being able to follow argument, do you think that is a good reason for not being able to stand trial?

A. That is one reason.

Q. What other reasons are there?

A. In my opinion he is a mentally sick person.

Q. What is his intelligence; or what is his I.Q.?

A. Very high.

Q. Do you know what it is?

A. Something over 120. There has been no impairment of the intelligence over the years. That again is a characteristic of the disorder we are describing. Paranoids are very apt to develop among those of high intelligence whereas the schizophrenics are more likely to occur in individuals with low I.Q.

Q. By schizophrenic you mean a person with a split personality, do you not?

A. Yes.

Q. That a person is a schizophrenic in and of itself does not mean that he is not able to stand trial?

A. No, not at all. However, very early it was my impression that he should not be classified as a psychotic or insane person and, therefore, should not be absolved from the necessity of standing trial, but during subsequent examinations and interviews my view was changed because it became obvious, after talking to him for long periods of time, that much of his talk was definitely abnormal.

Q. It would make a difference, though, would it not, if any attorney, who was skilled in such matters, were attempting to get a direct answer from him rather than one who was not?

A. I think so.

Q. Could you get a direct answer if you insisted on it?

A. I don't know.

Q. Did you insist on a direct answer any time?

A. Oh, yes.

Q. And did you get answers direct?

A. Sometimes, yes.

Q. Did he tell you why he was brought over to the United States?

A. Yes.

Q. What did he say?

A. He declared that he had the feeling if he gave himself up and volunteered to come to this country that he would really be welcome because of the valuable information which he had which would be helpful in dealing with our enemies, but that after he was cast into confinement at Pisa he felt that he had been very definitely mistreated and double-crossed; and when he was brought to the United States he again felt that even though he came in the capacity of a prisoner, still and all there must be some way out so that he could divulge what he knew to the proper people. By the proper people he meant pretty high officials. He was willing to come for that reason. He felt that there were elements against him, perhaps commandos and British Secret Service, and even others involved in this double-cross proposition.

Q. Did he say when he first learned that he was charged with treason?

A. I think it was while he was in Pisa.

Q. And why did he give himself up? What did he think he was charged with? What was the purpose of giving himself up?

A. I don't know for sure, but I suppose he knew that he was to be apprehended as soon as possible. I don't know for sure.

Q. Do you know what he knew about that?

A. No.

Q. Or when he knew he was charged with treason?

A. No, I don't recall that.

MR. ANDERSON: That is all.

Redirect Examination

BY MR. CORNELL:

Q. Doctor, you mentioned having read some of his poetry which seemed to you rational and poetic.

A. I didn't pay much attention to it.

Q. Did you make any comparison between his early and late poetry in that respect?

A. Well, I saw one of his poems, that he had prepared in the camp at Pisa which, of course, was incoherent and impossible for me to understand, as compared with the earlier.

Q. The poems you found coherent were earlier, is that right?

A. Yes.

Q. During cross-examination you said that you considered his distractibility and deficiency in speech. Did you or the other doctors make any examination to determine if that same tendency was disclosed in his writing? Having in mind that he is a man of great literary ability, did you determine whether he was affected in his writing?

A. Yes, he was, and he feels that due to fatigue and exhaustion that it would be impossible for him to write very much at the present time.

Q. In other words, he told you he could not write at the present time?

A. That is right, and I believe it.

Q. Does the fact that he is a man of high intelligence have anything to do with his ability to understand and reason logically with regard to this offense?

A. It would have if he were not afflicted with this paranoid reaction, but that is fixed to such an extent that he cannot reason in an intelligent manner.

Q. Being intelligent, then, does not help him?

A. That is right.

MR. CORNELL: That is all.

MR. ANDERSON: Doctor, just one question—a person may be abnormal along one line and yet be normal on other lines, might he not?

THE WITNESS: He could have false ideas on one line, yes.

MR. ANDERSON: That is all.

(Witness excused.)

eleven

Morning and Afternoon:

Dr. Winfred Overholser

MR. CORNELL: Call Dr. Overholser.

Thereupon—

DR. WINFRED OVERHOLSER

was called as a witness for and on behalf of the Defendant, and being first duly sworn, was examined and testified as follows:

THE CLERK OF THE COURT: Be seated, please, and state your full name.

THE WITNESS: My name is Winfred Overholser.

Direct Examination

BY MR. CORNELL:

Q. Dr. Overholser, will you tell me your profession at the present time?

A. I am Superintendent of St. Elizabeths Hospital in this city.

Q. You are the chief medical officer of that hospital?

A. Yes.

Q. What is the relation of that hospital to the United States Government?

A. It is operated entirely by the Federal Government under the Federal Security Agency.

Q. Is there any other hospital in the District of Columbia which is a mental hospital?

A. The psychiatric division of Gallinger Hospital.

Q. That is a division of the general hospital?

A. Yes.

Q. Your hospital is purely mental?

A. Yes.

Q. How many patients do you have?

A. Just under seven thousand.

Q. How many doctors are directly serving under you?

A. Approximately fifty, with some vacancies.

Q. How long have you been in charge of the institution?

A. Since October, 1937.

Q. In what professional capacity were you engaged prior to that time?

A. I was Commissioner of Mental Diseases in Massachusetts until December, 1936.

Q. Were you then chief medical officer of Massachusetts with reference to mental diseases?

A. I was head of the department which administered ten hospitals.

Q. Prior to that?

A. I had served in various capacities in the State hospital service from July, 1917, on, except some time I was in the Army Medical Corps.

Q. During all this time you have been connected with psychiatric work and public health, is that right?

A. Psychiatric work, yes.

Q. How long have you been practicing medicine?

A. I was graduated in 1916 from Chicago University.

Q. Are you the author of any textbooks or scientific articles?

A. Scientific articles.

Q. Will you tell us what examination you have made of Ezra Pound?

A. I was requested to serve with Dr. King and Dr. Gilbert of Gallinger to advise the Chief Justice on the condition of the defendant after the defendant was committed to Gallinger Hospital for observation.

Q. The request came from Chief Justice Laws?

A. Yes. I saw him on several occasions; I saw him alone twice, and I saw him with all of the other doctors at one date and another, and we made a report December 15, when we had Dr. Muncie with us in order that we might be talking about the same thing.

Q. What was your conclusion in that report?

A. It was our opinion that the defendant was unfit mentally and unable to stand trial.

Q. And then since that date he has been in your hospital?

A. He was admitted to St. Elizabeths on January 1, and has been there ever since.

Q. Has he been under constant observation?

A. Yes, he has been under constant observation. I spent a long time in consultation with him and other doctors last Thursday, and I have before me the report made by the other physicians at that hospital, and I see no reason to change my opinion.

Q. Will you tell us the reasons which lead you to the conclusion that he is unable to participate in the trial of this indictment intelligently?

A. Of course, in the first place we have the background of his history and the Department of Justice has been very helpful in making available what files they have concerning the case.

Q. Do you remember before that, or had you seen the text of his alleged broadcasts?

A. Yes, and other things in addition. In the first place, it is quite obvious that the man has always been unusually eccentric through the years. He has undoubtedly a high regard of his own opinion, and has been extremely vituperative of those who disagree with him.

He has a very high degree of intelligence, there is no question on that score, and his relations with the world and other people during practically all his life have been those of a person who was very skeptical to say the least.

He is extremely free in his conversation; he has not been reticent by any stretch of the imagination, but his production has been unusually hard to follow. He speaks in bunches of ideas.

Q. You mean his production of speech?

A. Yes, and rambling and illogical.

There was an episode shortly after he was taken into custody by the American Forces in Italy during which he was extremely agitated and anxious, and he has shown episodes such as that sometimes when he was under observation both at Gallinger and St. Elizabeths. At times he has been extremely restless, and at times his speech has been more disconnected than others.

The ideas, perhaps, which he expresses indicate some of his views in connection with the war. In the first place, he is thoroughly convinced that if he had been allowed to send his messages to the Axis, which he wished to send, prior to 1940, there would have been no Axis even. In other words, that if given a free hand by those who were engaged in stultifying him, he could have prevented the war.

He lays a great deal of his difficulty at the door of British Secret Service, and other groups, which have opposed him.

He assures me, too, that he served a very useful purpose to the United States by remaining at the Italian prison camp to complete his translation of Confucius, which he regards as the greatest contribution to literature.

He is sure that he should not have been brought to this country in the capacity of a prisoner, but in the capacity of someone who was to be of great benefit to the United States in its post-war activities.

I might state that this constitutes a grandiosity of ideas and be-

liefs that goes far beyond the normal, even in a person who is as dis-
traught in his mind as he is.

From a practical view of his advising with his attorney, there
would be the fact that you cannot keep him on a straight line of
conversation; he rambles around, and has such a naive grasp of the
situation in which he finds himself, it would not be fair to him or
his attorney to put him on trial.

Furthermore, due to the episode he had in Pisa when he was
under confinement, I think there would be a much more violent
reaction on top of this paranoid reaction if the trial was to proceed.

Q. You mentioned his naive reasoning. Will you expand on
that?

A. For example, he did not expect to be brought here. He did
not expect to be put in prison when he got here. He thought he
was to be used by the government in any movement for the organization of the world. He is sure that his connections with Japan
would enable him to deal with the delicate post-war situation. I
think "naive" is a mild word to apply to that line of reasoning.

Q. Based upon your knowledge and understanding of the situation, how do you regard his ability to understand the situation and
to answer questions in connection with the presentation of his
defense?

A. Well, with an infinite amount of patience, and an infinite
amount of time, it might be possible sometime in the future to get
a lucid answer to a question.

Q. In other words, would his discursiveness and inability to
answer questions prevent his attorney from presenting his side of
the picture in defense of this indictment?

A. It would.

MR. CORNELL: Your witness.

THE COURT: Just a minute, I have to attend a meeting.

Members of the jury, do not talk to anyone about this case, and
do not permit anyone to talk to you about it, and please do not
discuss it among yourselves until I submit it to you. Be back at 2
o'clock.

MR. CORNELL: Your Honor, may Dr. Muncie be excused?

THE COURT: Yes, he may be excused.

(Thereupon, at 12:30 o'clock p.m., Court was recessed and further proceedings herein continued until 2 o'clock p.m., Wednesday, February 13, 1946.)

The afternoon session began with the cross-examination of Dr. Overholser. He had barely finished talking about Pound's "blow-ups," when the defendant had one of them. The triggering word was "Fascism."

(Pursuant to recess heretofore taken, Court was reconvened at 2 o'clock p.m., Wednesday, February 13, 1946, and the following occurred:)

THE COURT: You may proceed.

Thereupon—

DR. WINFRED OVERHOLSER,

a witness heretofore called on behalf of the defendant, being re-called, and having been heretofore sworn, resumed the stand and testified further as follows:

Cross-Examination

BY MR. MATLACK:

Q. Doctor, I understood you to say that you based your opinion partly on your own observation and partly on examination of records at the hospital.

A. That is right.

Q. Do you have with you the records of the hospital showing his present condition?

A. Yes, sir.

Q. Could you produce them?

A. Surely; it is in my briefcase.

Q. Have you, yourself, treated Mr. Pound, or has that been left to your associates out there?

A. Partly to the associates.

Q. Are these records the records made by the staff?

A. That is right.

Q. And will you state by referring to them what the records show as to his present state of mental health?

A. It is a rather bulky record, as you see.

Q. Can you summarize it?

A. Essentially it is that there has been very little change in his condition since he came in. A summary of the case from the time he came in is pretty much in line with what I said this morning, and the whole staff has seen him. There has been some discussion about him which has not been formal; in fact, there has been no formal diagnosis they have made as yet.

Q. No formal diagnosis?

A. No.

Q. What is your opinion as to the chances of improvement for this patient?

A. As far as the basic sub-strata beneath those ideas of persecution, and so on, I should say not particularly good.

The matter of the secondary "blow-up," so to speak, if I may use that slang expression, is not particularly important, and while he is in this particular condition I do not look for any fundamental change in his condition.

Q. By these blow-ups—

A. These quiet states I think are more or less reaction to the stresses under which he may be placed. They are to my mind secondary. Fundamentally we are dealing with a paranoid condition, which I usually have found tends to progress rather than otherwise.

Q. Now, if he does not have these blow-ups, as you call them—I am going to use that expression, I think it is descriptive—where he is in those quiet states, would you say that during those periods he would be able to consult with counsel?

A. No, I don't think so, not for the purposes of which we are speaking now.

Q. Now, what part does his background history play in your opinion as to his present sanity?

A. It shows that we are dealing now with the end-product of an individual who throughout his lifetime has been highly antagonistic, highly eccentric, the whole world has revolved around him, he has been a querulous person, he has been less and less able to order his life. This has been a gradual evolution through his life, so that now we are dealing with the end-product, so to speak.

Q. Do you think that because he is eccentric that makes him unable to consult counsel?

A. Oh, no.

Q. That is true of many people?

A. Yes.

Q. That does not make him unable to consult with counsel?

A. It might make him a nuisance.

Q. Make him a nuisance but not insane?

A. Yes.

Q. I think you said one of the characteristics was that he was very vituperative to one who opposed his will?

A. He has been.

Q. Do you think that, in itself, displays a person who could not be able to consult with counsel?

A. Not in itself. I haven't said that any one of these things in itself would.

Q. I am going to come to that. I have forgotten what other thing you did say. I did understand you to say that he is vituperative, and eccentric; I don't know whether you used the word "sensitive" or not.

A. No, but he is highly supersensitive.

Q. Now, couldn't a man who was eccentric, and vituperative, and all the other attributes that you have given to him rolled into one, still be able to consult with counsel?

A. Even with all those three, and with nothing else, very likely, yes.

Q. I understand that what we are concerned with in this inquiry is not the question of the difference between right and wrong, that is, as to being able to distinguish between right and wrong, but whether he is able to consult with counsel and conduct a defense.

A. That is correct.

Q. Did he give you in his general history anything about his belief in Fascism?

A. I did not discuss that with him particularly.

THE DEFENDANT: I never did believe in Fascism, God damn it; I am opposed to Fascism.

BY MR. MATLACK:

Q. I don't know whether you answered the question, or not.

THE COURT: I think he answered it.

BY MR. MATLACK:

Q. Did he ever discuss with you his advocacy of Mussolini and his politics?

A. In the most general terms. I didn't go into that in great detail, either. I looked upon that as a political matter.

Q. Well, that is what I am beginning to get at. Did you read his book entitled Jefferson and Mussolini?

A. No.

Q. Did you take into consideration the fact that living in Italy, where the political philosophy was Fascism, that he may have become imbued with that philosophy?

MR. CORNELL: Your Honor, I object to this line of questioning and characterization of Mr. Pound, which I think is very distressing to him.

THE COURT: I will give you a certain latitude, but try not to disturb him if you can help it.

MR. MATLACK: I will strike the question and ask it again.

BY MR. MATLACK:

Q. Did the fact that living in Italy, where Fascism was a political philosophy, and where most of the people in Italy had adopted the Mussolini Government, have any influence, do you think, on the question of whether he is sane or insane?

A. No, I should not say so.

Q. Well, would the fact that somebody believed like Mussolini in his theories, or political philosophies, and the fact that others joined in his beliefs, and were otherwise normal, make them abnormal?

A. I think that is a question of politics rather than psychiatry.

Q. Now, on the same theory, if somebody believes in an economic theory such as social credit, and is able to write and broadcast his theories about social credit, does the fact that he is imbued with a belief in social credit, if he is otherwise normal, make him abnormal or insane?

A. I don't know that I mentioned his views on social credit. There are a great many people who take stock in that view of economics, but I do not think that because one believes in it stamps him any more than out of agreement with most people in this country at least.

Q. If I understand your testimony, he has certain grandiose ideas of saving the Constitution through the money clause in the Constitution, and that on certain economic theories if he could get to Japan he might have been of some service to the United States, and so on; I think that is what you testified to.

A. I am not sure on the economic phase of the theories and, in fact, I never did get to the end of the explanation.

Q. Now, just how was he going to save the Constitution.

A. There was some discussion about the money clause of the Constitution, but just what it had to do with saving the Constitution I was not quite clear.

Q. How does the fact that your conclusion is based on a paranoid state, if—

A. I didn't say that; I couldn't get his explanation on that particular point.

Q. On what do you base your conclusion that he is in a paranoid state if it isn't based on his theories about saving the Constitution, and so on?

A. The matter of his saving the Constitution, the mention about saving the Constitution is one of the factors. I don't remember that I mentioned that. I did mention particularly his idea that he could have prevented the formation of the Nazis; that he was the victim of machinations of the British Secret Service and antagonistic groups; that he was of far more use as an adviser to the Government than as a defendant in a criminal case.

Q. Did you ascertain what information he claimed to have that would be of such benefit to the Government?

A. There was some discussion of it in an excursive and rambling way. I must say I was not impressed by the flow of the conversation. That is one of the reasons he asked us to—

Q. On the other hand, you think that under those circumstances, he thought he would be of service to the United States?

A. As I say, he was unable to explain what that was, or how it would be accomplished. It was the fact he felt he was so important and of such value to the United States that I put him down as suffering a mental disorder.

Q. Did you talk to him at all about the charge of treason he is under?

A. Yes.

Q. Did he understand that he had done anything treasonable?

A. Apparently not, because he denied that he had done anything in connection with the Government of Italy against the United States. There was no significance apparently to that charge.

Q. Did he feel that because he did not think he had committed a treasonable act would make him an innocent man?

A. No.

Q. Isn't it a fact that people charged with crime do that?

A. Yes.

Q. And that doesn't make him innocent?

A. No.

Q. Do you think he thought he understood what treason meant?

A. I should say in a general way.

Q. Did he realize that he was subject to trial and possible conviction and punishment?

A. I should say that his attitude was that the reasons for his being brought over as a prisoner was a part of the plot against him on the part of the British Secret Service and the Communist groups that he mentioned; in other words, that they were instigating the Department of Justice in the prosecution. That sounded to me pathological.

Q. Do you think that that could be without any foundation of fact when shortly before that he had given a statement to the Department as to his activities in which he recognized that he had been charged with treason?

A. Oh, he knew he had been charged with treason. He told me that.

Q. And he knew it before he was brought to this country?

A. Oh, yes.

Q. But did I understand you to say that notwithstanding that, that he thought he was coming over here to be of assistance to the United States in some other capacity?

A. Yes.

Q. Do you think that that was something he might have told you out of whole cloth?

A. It did not appear that way to me; taking into consideration the whole line of examination, I am quite convinced that there was no question of malingering.

Q. No malingering in that statement or any other, but in that particular statement you did not think that there was any question of malingering?

A. No.

Q. Is your opinion based at all on the fact that the crime with which he is charged is closely tied up with his profession of writing? By that I mean the treason charge is the broadcasting and writing of manuscripts and broadcasting information to the United States, which is in line, that is, the written part of it is in line with his life's work? Do you base your opinion at all on the fact that he is charged with treason and that he has a psychosis, fear of apprehension?

A. Will you please ask that again? Your question is not quite clear. You are asking whether this psychosis is due entirely to the fact that he is in this situation under indictment for a serious offense?

Q. That's right.

A. No, I don't think so.

Q. You think that if he was not under arrest in a concentration camp or was, as he described, under arrest for treason, he would still have the same psychosis?

A. He may not have believed it, possibly; those are secondary pretty much, but they are secondary.

Q. Do you think that he suffers from delusions of any kind?

A. Yes.

Q. What delusions do you say he suffers from?

A. Well, I think they are both delusions of grandeur and delusions of persecution, both of which are characteristic of what we call the paranoid condition.

Q. You don't say that he suffers with paranoia though?

A. I will say it is a paranoid condition; the distinctions between paranoia, schizophrenia and one thing and another run into each other, but it resembles paranoia, if you wish to put it that way.

Q. Do you feel that he was so imbued with his economic theories, or whatever his message might have been, that even if he had realized the consequences of his treasonable act that he still would have broadcast?

A. I haven't an opinion on it.

MR. MATLACK: I think that is all.

MR. CORNELL: I would like to ask one or two questions.

Redirect Examination

BY MR. CORNELL:

Q. Doctor, you said that as to a number of specific delusions and specific deviations from the normal which you found in this case, that each one of those by itself would not necessarily indicate the opinion which you have given?

A. Yes.

Q. However, would it not be true in any psychiatric investigation that one single instance of abnormality taken by itself would not indicate a conclusion one way or the other?

A. Just as two lines do not make a picture.

Q. All must be considered together in order to arrive at a conclusion?

A. That is correct.

Q. And when you do consider, not piecemeal but jointly, the points you have mentioned, your opinion is that the man suffers from the disease you described?

A. That is correct.

Q. Would you say also, apart from your diagnosis, and apart from expressing any opinion with regard to sanity or insanity in the usual medical parlance, that the inability to understand and concentrate on the part of this individual was such that he could not participate in a trial?

A. That is correct.

Q. So that all these eccentricities and abnormalities, and the medical diagnosis based on them, could be ignored, and still you would say because of the way this man reacts to questioning and reasoning, he still is unable to defend himself in this trial?

A. These secondary situations standing by themselves would probably disqualify him from a proper trial, but I should prefer not even to segregate it even the way you do, but to keep the whole picture.

Q. Perhaps this is a broad question to get an opinion on, but even if you were not determined in your mind as to the reasons which underlie the way in which he acts, would you not even then say that his reactions are such that he is not able to be tried, regardless of the diagnosis?

A. I suppose my answer would be yes to that. It is a rather complicated question, and again I do not like to duck the other part.

Q. Suppose you put yourself in my place as an attorney questioning a man accused of a crime; I know nothing about psychiatric diagnosis any more than the average layman, and may not be able to form an opinion as to these abnormalities but, nevertheless, I know from questioning the man that I can't get an answer out of him, putting yourself in the place of the layman would you be able to say this man is sufficiently able to reason and give coherent answers?

A. I think he is not.

Q. And that would be apparent even to a layman who did not understand medical conditions which brought this about?

A. I understand that it has been, and I certainly agree that it is the case.

MR. CORNELL: Thank you. That is all.

Redirect Examination

BY MR. MATLACK:

Q. But do I understand, Doctor, that you say he does have an understanding of the charge made against him, and an understanding of his position in relation thereto?

A. He understands in the sense that he knows it is a fact that he has been indicted for certain actions which are of a serious criminal nature. I am not so sure I would say that he understands fully his relation thereto; that is, he knows what his name is, and he knows a person by that name has been indicted for that offense, but he has a significant lack of comprehension of all the events to comprehend fully the situation in which he now is, although intellectually he knows that there is such a thing as treason in acts against the United States.

Q. He has that information?

A. He has an understanding intellectually which is different from appreciating his connection with that set of facts.

Q. Does he have any loss of memory as to the fact that he did write manuscripts and broadcast them?

A. He speaks of that. His memory on some things is quite uncertain. There was some discussion, I remember, of him having dictated some manuscripts for broadcasts.

Q. But he understands what he did?

A. In that sense, yes.

Q. Now, what is there about him that you say he cannot consult with his counsel when he understands the charge and understands what he did do?

A. He understands the charge as far as it implies to some abstract person. I do not think he comprehends or knows how that applies to this particular charge. That goes to his responsibility, and I am not discussing that, but I do say that his mental condition is such that he is unable to discuss with any degree of coherence the explanation for being in the situation in which he is, or his motive for so doing.

Q. Do you think his motivations and reasons for making the broadcasts have anything to do with his ability to tell his counsel what he did do?

A. I should think so.

Q. Is it because of that fact that you think he is unfit to consult with counsel?

A. Not wholly.

Q. Is it because you think anyone who has a paranoid state is unable to consult his counsel?

A. Not necessarily. I think I have indicated that in a situation he might very readily have one of these, can I say "blow-ups," again, during which he would be quite unable perhaps to concentrate enough to recognize the importance to his defense.

Q. Of what duration are those blow-ups?

A. Well, the one at Pisa lasted several weeks, as far as one can gather from the report of the psychiatrists there.

Q. What was this incident he told you happened at Pisa? I suppose he mentioned something to you. It has been mentioned here, and I think it should appear what it was, something he said?

A. I have seen the reports of the psychiatrists.

Q. Do you pass on the reports of psychiatrists?

A. No, not of those.

Q. What did Mr. Pound tell you?

A. In the first place, he was quite sure then, as he tells it now, that lies were told on him specifically. It is quite likely that that was not the case, that he was in a state of panic, that he was off in his memory after that; he says he can't remember details clearly of what went on there even; that he developed some curious headaches and was determined at that time to be suffering from an anxiety neurosis state, and was given a little more latitude for that reason.

Q. Have you seen the opinion of those psychiatrists?

A. Yes.

Q. What was that opinion?

A. That he had anxiety neurosis.

Q. Could that have anything to do with the present opinion of the doctors around here?

MR. CORNELL: I object to that.

MR. MATLACK: He said he based it on their opinion.

THE WITNESS: I don't think it has a great deal to do with my opinion, but I was asked about what went on in Pisa, and I wasn't in Pisa myself.

BY MR. MATLACK:

Q. You said you based it partly on reading those reports?

A. Yes.

Q. And then I asked you did those doctors find him insane?

A. They said he was not psychotic.

Q. That means he was not insane?

A. They were, I think, interested in prison facts.

Q. When they said he was not psychotic that means he was not insane?

A. That he was not suffering from a major mental disease. That was their impression. How long they saw him, I don't know, or what their experience was.

Q. Would you say that the incident known now as the Pisa incident was the result of one of those blow-ups?

A. Yes. Apparently he had been held incommunicado in an uncovered cage of some kind out in the yard, and that apparently developed a neurotic state because of that.

MR. MATLACK: That is all.

MR. CORNELL: That is all.

MR. MATLACK: If the Court please, may Dr. Overholser be excused? Mr. Cornell says he has no objection.

THE COURT: Yes.

(Witness excused.)

Dr. Overholser left the court with his bulky briefcase. In it were reports disagreeing with his own findings, made by young doctors on the staff of St. Elizabeths who thought that Pound was merely eccentric and wanted to see him tried.

Mr. Matlack, as we have seen, did not ask Dr. Overholser to produce the reports.

twelve

Afternoon Session:

Dr. Joseph L. Gilbert

MR. CORNELL: Will you call Dr. Gilbert?

Whereupon—

DR. JOSEPH L. GILBERT,

a witness called on behalf of the Defendant, being first duly sworn, was examined and testified as follows:

THE CLERK OF THE COURT: Be seated, please, and state your full name.

THE WITNESS: Dr. Joseph L. Gilbert.

Direct Examination

BY MR. CORNELL:

Q. Will you tell what your official position is at the present time?

A. I am chief psychiatrist, Gallinger Municipal Hospital.

Q. That is in the District of Columbia?

A. Washington, District of Columbia.

Q. And do you have charge of all the mental patients in that institution?

A. I have charge of that department.

Q. Supervision of it?

A. Yes.

Q. How long have you held this position?

A. Fifteen years next April 1.

Q. During that time have you devoted yourself exclusively to psychiatry?

A. Yes, and for some years before that.

Q. How many years have you specialized in that branch of medicine?

A. I began my training in psychiatry in 1923, and then began to devote my entire time to psychiatry two years later, at the end of 1925, and entirely after January 1, 1926, on the staff of St. Elizabeths until April 1, 1931.

Q. How did you happen to become connected with this case?

A. Well, Mr. Ezra Pound was admitted to the psychiatric department for mental observation December 3, 1945, and either shortly before or after the time of Mr. Pound's admission, I was directed by my superintendent, at the request of Dr. King of the Bureau of Prisons, Department of Justice, to join in the examination, I believe incident to a direction of this Court.

Q. And you and Dr. King and Dr. Overholser were jointly requested by the Court to make the examination, is that correct?

A. That was my understanding, and I think through Dr. King.

Q. Now, when did you first examine Mr. Pound? Was it immediately upon his admission to your hospital?

A. Not immediately. The first formal examination was on December 6, and then December 12 or December 13 formally, and at other times brief interviews during Mr. Pound's residence in the psychopathic department of Gallinger up to December 21.

Q. He was there, then, from December 3 to December 21?

A. 1945.

Q. And you saw him regularly during that period?

A. I saw him but not with any regularity, but at rather frequent intervals and on the dates specified for the purpose of formal examination.

Q. Did you also cause any investigation to be made by members of your staff during the times when he was not under your direct eye?

A. We had some special examinations, not entirely special either, but some routine examinations made by some of the junior members of the staff, such as the taking of the blood plasm, a certain examination of the chest, and a special examination at my request of the genito-urinary system.

Q. Did you find any evidence from these physical examinations which would give any indication one way or the other as to his mental health?

A. No, sir; the physical examinations were almost entirely negative, including X-rays, blood examination and genito-urinary examination.

Q. By "negative," do you mean they showed him to be normal in those respects?

A. Relatively normal, yes, sir; no significant physical findings.

Q. After he left your hospital on December 21 did you have occasion to examine him further?

A. Yes, sir; I examined him again, and the last time on February 7 at St. Elizabeths Hospital.

Q. Is that the only occasion since December 21 that you examined him?

A. That's right.

Q. And that examination was in conjunction, was it, with the three doctors who have testified here?

A. That's right.

Q. Now, will you tell us what your diagnosis was of his state based on your investigation?

A. Yes, sir; as the result of my examinations of Mr. Pound during the period of observation in Gallinger, and on the date specified of the making of the examination of February 7, 1946, at St. Elizabeths Hospital, it is my opinion that Mr. Pound is of unsound mind and suffering from a paranoid state.

Q. Now, we are not very much more enlightened than we were before because I take it you will agree that these are not terms of great exactitude. I would like to have you tell us what things he exhibits of significance in this picture.

A. Well, a paranoid state is not uncommon and is a well recognized mental disorder that is characterized in the beginning in a fair number of cases by what is known as the hypochondriacal stage of the disorder that may last for a longer or shorter period of time, usually rather prolonged, and during which the patient has a great many strange systemic symptoms, or symptoms referrable to the body, or any part of the body, and about which the person is concerned, and will inquire of the cause.

This period of illness may continue over several years, and following which the person moves into what is known as a persecutory state, or phase of the disease that may, not always, but may be characterized by delusions of persecution which may, in turn, be supplanted by delusions of grandeur, that is, delusions of self-importance, and the delusions of persecution may to some extent diminish, or the disorder may continue to be characterized by the delusions of persecution and delusions of grandeur, or delusions of self-importance. One or the other may be in preponderance, that is, one may overshadow the other, that is, the delusion of grandeur, or the delusions of persecution, and in some of the cases that are classified as paranoid states the disorder may subside for a considerable period of time, but more frequently remains a chronic type of mental disorder.

Q. You have been telling us what you mean by the term "paranoid" but not attempting to describe this particular individual, is that right?

A. The major symptoms of a paranoid state or paranoid psychosis.

Q. That is what you have been giving?

A. Yes.

Q. Now, did you find in this defendant the symptoms you mentioned of hypochondriasis and delusions of grandeur?

A. Yes.

Q. Can you give us an illustration of how he is hypochondriac?

A. On the various occasions of my examining him, when I have seen him he has complained that for at least four years he has felt unusually fatigued, and in describing that condition, rather he attempts to describe that condition by stating that his ability for a number of years on the work he has undertaken to, and did undertake to attend to while reclining in bed, and that when those symptoms of fatigue are more marked he describes his feeling at the time as being unable to get flat enough in bed, and then during the various examinations he spoke of this fatigue and exhaustion very frequently, and more or less—I mean it was consistent, it was present all of the time he was interviewed, whether for a short or long period.

While he was in the psychiatric department of Gallinger he remained in bed practically all of the time with the possible exception of sitting up for his meals, or going to a bathroom nearby, and during long periods of interviews with him he remained reclining in bed, with the additional symptom of restlessness, rather rapid movements about the bed, and suddenly sitting or rising to the upright sitting position, or to move quickly about from the bed to a table nearby to get some paper, book or manuscript, and then to as suddenly throw himself on the bed and again assume the reclining position. This fatigue and exhaustion, which he states was completely reducing him, as he said, to the level of an imbecile in his thinking capacity, was notwithstanding the fact that he was undergoing no amount of physical activity. His thinking and mental activities were so greatly interfered with during the long or short periods of interviews that he easily, and a number of times during longer periods became quite exhausted, emotionally and physically, too.

Along with that was a certain amount of rather marked restlessness notwithstanding the reclining position in bed, and quick movements either into bed, or movements of experimentation, or movements to assume the sitting position, or movements to secure a book, a sheet of paper, or other articles in the room, in an agitated type of physical activity.

He spoke of his mental processes being in a fog, to use his own words, that he admits during these periods of severe fatigue that he was unable to undertake temporarily any mental activity, and also complained of pressure throughout various regions of the head, what he described as a feeling of hollowness, going through this gesture (indicating) with his fingers, describing the vortex of the skull, indicating that there was a feeling not only of pressure but of hollowness in that particular part of the cranium.

Q. Can you say whether in having him describe his symptoms and attitudes to you that there was any suspicion whatever of malingering, or did he appear to be entirely open and truthful about it?

A. I did not feel that there was any element of conscious malingering in any of the symptoms that were expressed during my various examinations of him.

I have not so far gone into what might be called the purely psychiatric symptoms, but I did not feel that there was any conscious element of malingering.

Q. In other words, he may not himself have been testifying about his true physical condition, but the things he told you he actually believed to be true?

A. Yes, I think that is correct.

Q. And can you tell us how he reacted to questioning about his predicament, about this indictment? Was he coherent and logical in his answers to questions, and his ability to understand the situation?

A. Well, if I may qualify the answer a bit instead of answering yes or no.

Q. I do not want a yes or no answer. I would like to have you tell us what you found in your own way.

A. When interrogating Mr. Pound for either short or long periods, it was exceedingly difficult to secure from him answers even to some of the simpler questions that were not rambling, occasionally irrelevant and extremely inconsistent. In other words, his answers, when obtained, and rather frequently answers were not obtained, to simple questions, his conversation was rambling and inconsistent, and at times very irrelevant.

Then, in fact, he would during his attempt to answer questions go into such rambling discourses on matters that had no relation to the question that he would lose the question and never get back to it, and even if I called him back to the question it was very frequently the case that you do not get a direct answer, or even any answer, that would be at all normal in certain phases, certain parts of the examination.

Then in addition there were at times rather marked outbursts, mental outbursts accompanied by profanity, not infrequently vulgarisms of one sort or another, with quite a strong tinge of hostility in certain phases of the examination that were at least inappropriate.

Q. Do you think that by reason of these reactions he would be able intelligently to consult with counsel sufficiently to defend against this indictment?

A. I feel that by reason of his mental disorder, he is unable to consult intelligently with counsel to defend himself in any action pertaining to the present case.

Q. You mentioned a number of instances about his personality which are abnormal. Can you point to any particular indications which led you to that conclusion, or is it based on an over-all diagnosis?

A. Yes, my conclusions are based on what I believe to be the presence of this not uncommon mental disorder, together with the abnormal additional content that I believe is present, leading to such extremely poor judgment that he would be unable to provide to counsel accurate or correct information that it would be necessary to give him at the time.

Q. Did you find, nevertheless, that he has an intellectual understanding of the nature of what he did, and of the fact that treason consists in certain violations? In other words, does he know what the law is, and does he recall his acts?

A. I am sure that he recalls his acts very clearly, but it is my opinion that his motive, and motives for the act are of abnormal origin; in other words, resulting from abnormal thinking.

Q. Do you think he is able to judge his acts in relation to this crime with sufficient dispassion and freedom from those eccentric attitudes, so that he could put himself in the place of his counsel, or the jury, and to understand or be able to formulate his defense, or, on the other hand, are his acts so cloudy that he is unable to consider it with proper balance?

A. I think the latter is true.

Q. Do you think that would prevent him from being able to stand trial under this indictment?

A. Yes, to the degree, as I have stated, that he would be unable to cooperate in a defense, to cooperate and understand; nor could he cooperate, with the thinking that goes along with his various ideas, for his act or acts have been based on abnormal type of thinking away beyond what might be considered as a mistake or error, even mistake in judgment or error in judgment, far beyond that.

MR. CORNELL: Thank you, Doctor. You may examine.

Cross-Examination

BY MR. ANDERSON:

Q. Dr. Gilbert, on these various occasions that you have mentioned on which you examined Mr. Pound, about how much time did you spend on each one of those?

A. It would only be possible for me to estimate that roughly in hours, perhaps a total of somewhere between eight and twelve hours.

Q. And was that divided approximately equally according to the number of times?

A. No, sir, some interviews were short, and then there were probably interviews not included in the eight to twelve hours when I saw him alone and not in conjunction with the other examiners.

Q. And, as I understand it, your opinion is based on your conversations with Mr. Pound and upon physical examinations that were made under your direction?

A. Well, based on the history obtained, the mental symptoms that in my opinion are present, and that in my opinion also are not based on any physical disorder or physical phenomena, but in conjunction with which sufficient physical examination was made to determine fairly accurately his general physical condition.

Q. Did you talk with him with reference to his life history?

A. Yes, sir.

Q. And did you also have documents or papers showing his life history, or information furnished from other sources to show his life history?

A. Yes, I had that.

Q. And did the two correspond, or was there any difference in the two?

A. Not any great difference in the factual data regarding his life history.

Q. He knew where he was born, in the State of Idaho, and when, and where he had resided, where he had gone to school, and the various places he had been without any trouble in recalling those matters?

A. Well, I wouldn't say without any trouble, although I think he was fairly accurate in his statements in that regard.

During these various examinations that were conducted it would be necessary at times to discontinue the examinations for sometimes a short period, or sometimes a longer period, by reason of the exhaustion and fatigue of which I have spoken, and of which Mr. Pound complained and was, in my opinion, present to a rather extreme degree.

Q. Would his age have anything to do with his becoming exhausted?

A. I believe not to the extent of which he complained. Furthermore, the physical examination failed to reveal, and it is my opinion that there are no serious physical handicaps; that for his sixty years, and slightly over, that he is in at least as good, if not better, physical condition than the average sixty-year-old. In other words, the fatigue and exhaustion of which he complains, as far as I could ascertain, were out of all proportion to any physical defects, which were only slight.

Q. And his mental intelligence is superior to the average individual of a like age, is it not?

A. Yes, sir, or any other age.

Q. But it would not be superior to his mental intelligence at the time he was probably twenty-eight or thirty years of age, would it?

A. His I.Q. was probably higher at a younger age, probably before the onset of this mental disorder.

Q. And what is his I.Q. at the present time?

A. I did not do the formal psychological, but I am sure the one who did it is a very competent person, and it is something slightly over 120, if I remember correctly.

Q. Was it done at Gallinger Hospital under your charge and direction?

A. Yes. Well, that is not exactly true. The psychologist who came was secured by Dr. King, through his service.

Q. I see.

A. Of the Bureau of Prisons.

Q. But it was done in the regular, customary manner that you follow at the institution?

A. Yes, sir, I am sure it was.

Q. You mentioned, I believe, Doctor, that Mr. Pound has grandiose ideas, and ideas of grandeur and ideas of persecution. Which is predominant in his case, if either is such?

A. Well, I haven't gone into this very much in detail, but it was my belief that after completing my examination that the delusions of grandeur were perhaps somewhat more in the foreground than other abnormal types of thinking.

Q. And what are delusions of grandeur?

A. Well, a delusion—I will have to break that up a little bit—is an idea not based on fact, not appropriate to the occasion, and not amenable to argument say, so a delusion of grandeur would be an idea of exaggerated importance, exaggerated self-esteem in his relation to the community, to the State, to the world as in this particular case.

Q. In case of a great person thinking themselves as great, is that a delusion of grandeur?

A. It may or may not be.

Q. And in case Mr. Pound thinks he is a great poet, would you say that is delusion of grandeur?

A. No, I did not consider that as one of his delusions of grandeur.

Q. What did you consider?

A. Well, his rather fixed belief that if certain circumstances had arisen that he would have been able to stop the formation of the so-called Axis and, therefore, have avoided the World War, and that if it had been possible for his writings to have reached the public, and especially important public officers throughout the world that the same thing would have happened, that the Axis would not have been formed, namely, the German-Italian-Japanese so-called Axis, and thereby the World War would have been prevented, and that there was a plot or conspiracy in certain quarters to prevent his writings from reaching the public, and especially certain important public officials he feels could have made use of his writings at the time and thereby have prevented the formation of the Axis and the World War; that he was interfered with in some way in setting up centers of learning where he also would have contributed to the prevention of the formation of the Axis and the World War; and that by his writings, his broadcasts, he was defending and saving the Constitution of the United States; that his economic theories were the last word in economy in the world, or in the economic field; that he believed he was being brought to America, after his imprisonment in Italy that he believed he was being brought to America for some use rather than—

Q. Rather than for trial?

A. Rather than to face an indictment or trial; that on one trip he made back here in about 1939 he made efforts to contact certain important people, or leaders in Congress, and that his efforts to do so were interfered with, and that had he been able to make those contacts, and others, that all of this that has happened could have been prevented; that he believed he could have contributed to that by going to Moscow to see Mr. Stalin.

Q. You think then, Doctor, that he has a hypochondriacal condition or state, do you?

A. Well, the medical diagnosis is paranoid state, in my opinion associated with the symptoms of delusions of grandeur more in the foreground than delusions of persecution, with the bodily symptoms, or so-called somatic symptoms, somatic meaning bodily, that I have described.

Q. Do you, or do you not, think that he has a hypochondriacal condition?

A. Not alone. Hypochondriasis is one entity in medicine that is rather well recognized, and with the symptoms I have spoken of I used the term, hypochondriacal state to describe the paranoid state, or paranoid condition.

Q. In your opinion is his condition something that came on suddenly or came on over a period of years, or does it get progressively worse or get progressively better?

A. Well, it is my opinion that it has been coming on for some years, and that the prognosis within the immediate future, or in a short period of time, is not favorable, that is, a recovery in a short period of time, in my opinion, is not to be expected.

Q. Did you discuss with Mr. Pound about how he lived in Italy, and what type of work he did, whether or not he wrote manuscripts, and if so what he did with them, and matters of that kind?

A. Yes, he had lived for more than twenty years at Rapallo, Italy, where he said he had been doing writing and research of one sort or another during that period that he lived there, and also during a period of some years before that he lived in London, also in Paris, but for more than twenty years in Rapallo, Italy, with the exception of one or two trips, one at least, to America, to the United States, and other trips the details of which I do not recall.

Q. Did he mention the fact that he had made radio broadcasts or recordings?

A. Yes, sir.

Q. And did he discuss all these matters clearly and intelligently?

A. No, sir; as a matter of fact, it was exceedingly difficult, if not impossible, to get from him anything approaching coherent or clear or concise answers about any of his activities, except to listen to his conversations, to the discourses I have described previously as rambling, and not infrequently irrelevant to try to pick out from that the essence in the form of factual data.

Q. Did Mr. Pound know he was charged with treason at the time you talked with him?

A. Yes, I am sure he did.

Q. Do you know when he first knew that?

A. No.

Q. Did he tell you whether or not anyone told him the purpose of coming to this country?

A. He may have said that he was told, but I do not recall his statement.

Q. Do you know where he got the basis for the belief that he was coming here to help the Government that you mentioned previously in your testimony?

A. Well, his belief regarding helping the Government goes back over a period of at least a few years when he believed he was defending and saving the Constitution by his broadcasts.

Q. Pardon me, Doctor, was your testimony to the effect that he was coming to the United States at this time in order to help the Government, or did I misunderstand?

A. He told me he believed he was being brought back to the United States, and I indicated that he thought he was coming back for some useful purpose rather than to face an indictment.

Q. And did he tell you where he got that belief?

A. No, sir.

Q. You don't know whether someone may have told him that for the purpose of making him an easy prisoner, do you?

A. No, sir, I do not, but I do not believe that is the case. I believe it is the outgrowth of his abnormal thinking.

Q. And do you believe he is able to comprehend what may be the outcome of a treason trial, should he be tried for treason?

A. To comprehend, yes, in a rather uncertain way he knows perhaps what would happen in case of his conviction on the charge.

Q. What causes you to believe he does in an uncertain way? Just what do you mean by that?

A. Well, in the first place he told me he thought he was being brought back so he could be made some use of, and during one of my earliest interviews with him he stated that he believed he was worth more to the country alive than dead.

Q. Did he say why?

A. Yes, at various times, and in a spotty manner, indicating that his knowledge of economic theories, of which he indicated he knew more than anyone else in the world, if they were applied to the world-wide situation even before the war or since.

Q. That could be a debatable question, could it not?

A. Well, as a principle it could well be a debatable question, but in the case of Mr. Pound, to my way of thinking, and according to my examination, it was my opinion that it was a delusion of grandeur.

Q. He also thought that he had not committed treason because under the Constitution he was granted the right of free speech?

A. Yes.

Q. Wouldn't that be a very good matter to present as a defense, or a possible defense?

A. I don't know, you are taking me into legal fields, now.

MR. CORNELL: Your Honor, I object to that. The witness isn't qualified to answer that.

THE COURT: I think that is probably correct.

BY MR. ANDERSON:

Q. In your opinion, Doctor, do you think he is entirely incompetent to consult counsel and properly, rationally give information to prepare his defense in this case?

A. I believe he is incompetent to do so.

Q. And you base your opinion upon what you have heretofore told us, do you, and also upon reading some of his works and writings?

A. Well, I based my opinion on the examination of the case. It is true I have seen some of his writings.

Q. Is it possible to reach an opinion in a matter of this kind with any degree of certainty, or is it more or less a question of various individuals reaching a different conclusion on the same set of facts?

A. That is rather involved, and I am afraid I might have to

speak for others there, but for myself I am not at all uncertain of my opinion in this case.

MR. ANDERSON: I think that is all, Doctor.

MR. CORNELL: That is all.

(Witness excused.)

MR. CORNELL: I rest, Your Honor.

MR. MATLACK: May we approach the bench?

THE COURT: Yes.

(Thereupon counsel approached the Court's bench and, out of the hearing of the jury, the following occurred:)

MR. MATLACK: You are not going to call Pound?

MR. CORNELL: I don't think so.

MR. MATLACK: I was going to ask the Court to call him as the Court's witness.

THE COURT: I don't think so. If we call him he will take two or three hours. I do not think it is necessary. The Court of Appeals says very plainly you cannot disregard an opinion of the psychiatrists.

MR. CORNELL: I am afraid he might blow up. He has been pretty nervous.

THE COURT: You don't want to argue the case, do you?

MR. CORNELL: No.

MR. MATLACK: No.

(Thereupon counsel retired to the trial table and, in the hearing of the jury, the following occurred:)

MR. CORNELL: I intend to make a motion for a directed verdict.

THE COURT: I will take the verdict, and so just for the record I will overrule it and note an exception.

Court's Charge to the Jury

THE COURT: Members of the Jury, there is a provision of our Code in the Laws of the District of Columbia to the effect that whenever a person is indicted for an offense, and before trial evidence is submitted to the judge that the accused is then insane the judge may cause a jury to be impanelled to inquire into the sanity or insanity of the accused, and if the jury shall find the accused to be then insane the Court may then bring about a commitment of the defendant to hospitalization, to remain in hospitalization until or unless there comes a time when it is found that he has recovered from his mental difficulties, and in that event he is certified back into the court for trial.

The reason for that law, of course, is obvious to all of us I am sure. It is absolutely essential that any person accused of the commission of a crime must be in a position to cooperate with counsel who is to defend him. He must understand the nature of the charges and be familiar and able to understand the offense which was alleged in the charge against him, to be able to tell the names of witnesses, what they might be able to say, and be able to give his own version to these acts which are alleged against him.

It is important, also, of course, that in the trial of the case that he be in position to cooperate with his counsel in his defense and, if he sees fit, if he chooses to take the stand, to testify understandingly and intelligently with regard to the facts in the case and to be cross-examined by the prosecution with regard to those facts and, of course, the law is humane to the extent that it does not want to bring about a person's breakdown at the trial of a criminal case if he is mentally ill and not able to stand the stress of a criminal trial.

In this particular case the defendant is charged with a serious offense, the offense of treason which, under certain conditions might result, if he is found guilty, in his punishment by electrocution, and when he was arraigned in court there was some suggestion made to me as the presiding judge that he was having mental difficulty, and on the strength of the showing that was then made, and later made in the form of affidavits, I committed him to Gallinger Hospital for examination.

It has been testified to before you correctly that we brought him to the point of having him examined by psychiatrists and physicians on mental diseases; we brought Dr. Overholser, who is the head of St. Elizabeths Hospital, one of the outstanding institutions of the United States, and run by the United States, and we brought to examine him also Dr. King who, as you have been told on the witness stand, holds a responsible position in the Public Health Service which attends to the mental as well as the physical condition of persons in the penal institutions throughout the United

States. We brought into consultation also Dr. Gilbert, who is the head of the Division of Psychiatry at Gallinger Hospital, with which I think you are doubtless familiar. Then there was permitted to examine him at the request of Mr. Cornell, who appeared for Mr. Pound, Dr. Muncie, who is a leading psychiatrist, and I think the head of the department at Johns Hopkins University. You heard his qualifications.

Those doctors, after consultation, filed a written certificate with the Court indicating their unanimous view that Mr. Pound under his then present state of mind was not in position to stand a trial, to cooperate with his counsel, and go through with a serious charge of this nature.

Government counsel have cooperated very readily in the investigation and were very fair in the entire situation and they, feeling that the code of law which I have explained to you should be complied with, filed in this court a motion that a jury be impanelled to pass upon this proposition. I agreed with the view of Government counsel that a jury be impanelled to look into it notwithstanding the unanimous opinion of these psychiatrists, and that is the reason why you have been impanelled today to hear the whole story, and those physicians have been questioned before you fully with regard to the situation.

It therefore becomes your duty now to advise me whether in your judgment you find that Mr. Pound is in position to cooperate with his counsel, to stand trial without causing him to crack up or break down; whether he is able to testify, if he sees fit, at the trial, to stand cross-examination, and in that regard, of course, you have heard the testimony of all these physicians on the subject, and there is no testimony to the contrary and, of course, these are men who have given a large part of their professional careers to the study of matters of this sort, who have been brought here for your guidance.

Under the state of the law you are not necessarily bound by what they say; you can disregard what they say and bring in a different verdict, but in a case of this type where the Government and the defense representatives have united in a clear and unequivocal view with regard to the situation, I presume you will have no difficulty in making up your mind. However it is my duty as the judge that whenever an issue is submitted to a jury to say to the jury that you are the sole judges of the facts, so when you retire to the jury room now select a foreman and try to make up your minds whether this defendant is presently of unsound mind, and when you make up your minds you answer the questions that the clerk will submit to you, and if you find that he is not of unsound mind you will return that kind of verdict.

Anything further?

MR. CORNELL: I think they should not draw any unfavorable inference due to the fact that Mr. Pound did not take the stand.

THE COURT: Counsel asked me with regard to that and I advised with them that I did not think it was necessary for him to take the stand, so you will not draw any unfavorable inference from that.

(The jury retired and returned after three minutes.)

THE CLERK OF THE COURT: Mr. Foreman, has the jury agreed upon its verdict?

THE FOREMAN OF THE JURY: It has.

THE CLERK OF THE COURT: What say you as to the respondent Ezra Pound? Is he of sound or unsound mind?

THE FOREMAN OF THE JURY: Unsound mind.

THE CLERK OF THE COURT: Members of the jury, your foreman says you find the respondent Ezra Pound of unsound mind, and that is your verdict so say you each and all?

(All members of the jury indicated in the affirmative.)

(Thereupon, the hearing was concluded.)

thirteen

Constitutional Questions

———————————— 1 ————————————

Pound was remanded to St. Elizabeths Hospital. His first lodging there was in Howard Hall—the "Hellhole," as he was to term it, a gloomy building with locked doors and barred windows inhabited by killers and rapists who had been adjudged insane. He was afterward transferred to Chestnut Ward, which operated under somewhat more ameliorating circumstances, and there he had a room to himself overlooking the Potomac. Mrs. Pound, who found herself stateless after the war, was finally permitted to come to the United States, and took a small apartment a few blocks from St. Elizabeths, where she was a daily visitor.

To the room where he wrote, and to the lawn where he held court, came famous callers, and a coterie of kooks who helped but little toward the final disposition of his case by their clamor. The letters poured forth again; forty-six of them went to a single correspondent and are described in a recent bookseller's catalogue as "inflammable" (on racial and political topics). Price for the lot: $3,750.

Pound also became the mentor by mail of a young man running for Congress from a midwestern state. His advice: "read Mein Kampf by the late Adolph HHHH houghton Mifflin—start on bit about 'public opinion' p. 85." He signed himself "Polonius." The passage, which covers several pages, is an attack on the press. More advice: "NEVER mention POWER/ from now on. Mendez technique: debauch, never interfere with lowest habits of electorate/ tell 'em they are free." Also: "denounce dictatorship and control monetary issue." Like a reflex action, the subject of money suggested another, and he recommended *The Defender*, an anti-Semitic publication—"after all, M. C. from [midwestern state] MUST represent a Christian public."

Pound's views aside, his confinement posed serious legal and constitutional questions. Although he had not been tried for treason—and consequently was not only not guilty but presumed to be innocent—his continued incarceration was, in effect, a life sentence. Mr. Cornell pressed these points upon Judge Laws in a new motion for bail, which was heard and denied on January 29, 1947, and in a petition for a writ of habeas corpus brought by Dorothy Pound, as Committee of the person and estate of Ezra Pound; this was filed February 11, 1948, and likewise denied. The points of law contained in them are not without interest. From the motion for bail:

Congress has provided that when a person charged with crime is found to be insane and unable to stand trial he may be confined in St. Elizabeths Hospital (24 U.S.C. Sec. 211). It is further provided that if such a person is restored to sanity he shall be returned to the court for trial. (24 U.S.C. Sec. 211b.) The law is silent, however, as to what should be done with a person who having been sent to St. Elizabeths Hospital is determined to be permanently insane but not to require permanent hospitalization.

Although the statute is silent on the point, if it should be construed so as to prevent release from St. Elizabeths Hospital of a person like the defendant who is found to be permanently insane, but not requiring hospitalization, then the statute would be unconstitutional. In the absence of medical grounds, a man may not be subjected to life imprisonment because an unprovable accusation has been brought against him. He would then be deprived of liberty without due process of law in violation of the Fifth Amendment to the United States Constitution.

It is respectfully submitted that based upon the medical opinions above referred to the defendant has a legal and constitutional right to be released from custody. If there is doubt as to the accuracy of medical opinion that he will never be restored to sanity, the court may retain control over the defendant by admitting him to bail and placing him in the care of a responsible physician. Bail is expressly permitted even in capital offenses (18 U.S.C. Sec. 597). It is therefore respectfully requested that the defendant be ordered released from St. Elizabeths Hospital and be admitted to bail and placed in the care of a private physician approved by the court.

The petition for the writ of habeas corpus is given in full:

Now comes DOROTHY POUND, as Committee of the person and estate of EZRA POUND, an incompetent person, and in behalf of EZRA POUND petitions this court as follows:

1. Petitioner is a citizen of the United States, domiciled in Italy, and temporarily sojourning in the District of Columbia, and is the wife of EZRA POUND.

2. On October 30, 1946, the petitioner was appointed by the District Court for the District of Columbia, Committee of the person and estate of EZRA POUND, who had been adjudged a person of unsound mind, and petitioner has duly qualified and is now acting as such Committee.

3. The petitioner asks for the issuance of a Writ of Habeas Corpus to determine the legality of the detention of EZRA POUND in the custody of the respondent, WINFRED OVERHOLSER, at St. Elizabeths Hospital, which is situated within the jurisdiction of this court and is under the direction of the respondent who is Superintendent thereof.

4. EZRA POUND is a United States citizen, domiciled in Italy, and has been confined in the District of Columbia since November 18, 1945, under indictment on the charge of treason against the United States. He was first confined in the District of Columbia jail, but was removed for medical examination to Gallinger Hospital, at the request of his attorney, JULIEN CORNELL, under order of this court dated November 27, 1945, which provided for an examination in regard to his sanity. Such examination was held and a report rendered to this court dated December 14, 1945, by the respondent and by DRS. JOSEPH L. GILBERT and MARION R. KING, both appointed by the court for making such ex-

amination, and by DR. WENDELL MUNCIE, employed by my husband's attorney, in which all four physicians joined in the opinion that my husband was of unsound mind and mentally unfit to advise properly with counsel, or to participate intelligently or reasonably in the defense of the charge of treason, and he was in need of care in a mental hospital. Following such report it was ordered by this court on December 21, 1945, that my husband, EZRA POUND, be sent to St. Elizabeths Hospital for treatment and examination, and he was forthwith removed to St. Elizabeths Hospital where he has since been continuously confined.

5. On January 18, 1946, this court, upon motion of the United States, ordered that a hearing be held to determine the sanity of EZRA POUND, in connection with the indictment for treason pending against him. The hearing was held on February 13, 1946, and medical testimony was received from DRS. OVERHOLSER, GILBERT, KING and MUNCIE above mentioned who reported that they had again examined my husband and on the basis of such examination and the previous examination, as well as observation of him in the interval, they all expressed the opinion that he was suffering from insanity of a paranoid type, which was of long duration, and that he would be unable properly to defend himself against the charge of treason, or to consult with counsel in his defense. At the conclusion of the testimony, a jury rendered a verdict that EZRA POUND was of unsound mind, and he was found by the court to be of unsound mind and remanded to St. Elizabeths Hospital.

6. On January 3, 1947, a motion was made by my husband's counsel for his admission to bail in order that he might be released from St. Elizabeths Hospital and privately treated. This motion was heard and denied by this court on January 29, 1947.

7. For a period of more than two years my husband has been under observation and treatment by the respondent, DR. WINFRED OVERHOLSER and his associates at St. Elizabeths Hospital. I know of my own knowledge and am informed by DR. OVERHOLSER that such treatment has not resulted in any improvement in my husband's mental condition. DR. OVERHOLSER informs me that in his opinion my husband will never recover his sanity, and there is no reasonable possibility that he will ever become mentally fit to stand trial.

8. In view of the fact that my husband appears to be permanently insane and can never be brought to trial under the indictment charging him with treason, I desire that he be released from St. Elizabeths Hospital and placed in my care. My attorney, JULIEN CORNELL, has consulted with DR. OVERHOLSER regarding the possibility of such release and has been informed by DR. OVERHOLSER that in his opinion my husband

does not require hospitalization; that his mental condition is of a mild nature which would permit him to be released from the hospital, and that he would benefit by the greater degree of freedom which would result from such release.

9. Although the respondent has expressed the opinion that my husband is permanently insane, and can never be brought to trial, and that he does not require hospitalization, the respondent, nevertheless, is unwilling and legally unable to release my husband from custody because he was committed to the respondent by order of this court.

10. If the court can rely upon DR. OVERHOLSER's opinion, and he is not only eminently qualified to determine such matters, but has also had the opportunity to keep my husband under continuous observation for a period of more than two years, then it appears that my husband is being held in custody, not because his illness or public safety requires his confinement, but solely because of the indictment which has been issued against him.

11. My husband, EZRA POUND, is held in custody pursuant to the authority of Section 211 of Title 24 of the United States Code which provides as follows:

"If any person, charged with crime, be found, in the court before which he is so charged, to be an insane person, such court shall certify the same to the Federal Security Administrator, who may order such person to be confined in Saint Elizabeths Hospital, and, if he be not indigent, he and his estate shall be charged with expenses of his support in the hospital."

12. The release from custody of persons so confined is provided in Section 211b of Title 24 of the United States Code which is as follows:

"When any person confined in Saint Elizabeths Hospital charged with crime and subject to be tried therefor, or convicted of crime and undergoing sentence therefor, shall be restored to sanity, the superintendent of the hospital shall give notice thereof to the judge of the criminal court, and deliver him to the court in obedience to the proper precept."

13. There is no provision in the statutes for the release from custody of a person who is found to be permanently insane and consequently unable to be tried, yet whose mental condition does not require confinement in a hospital or asylum. The statute does not prohibit release of

a person confined under such circumstances, but merely fails to make any provision to cover such an eventuality.

14. I am informed by counsel that my husband has the legal and constitutional right to be released from custody, because there is no justification in law for his continued confinement. When a person has been accused of crime and found to be of unsound mind, he may be properly confined for the reason that (1) there is an indictment pending against him under which he may be brought to trial if and when he recovers his sanity, or (2) his mental condition is such that he requires hospitalization, or (3) it would be dangerous to the public safety for him to remain at liberty. In the first case, the state is exercising its police power under which it may apprehend and confine persons awaiting trial while in the other case the state is acting as the guardian and *parens patriae* of persons who are unable to provide for their own welfare. But unless the state can properly bring to bear either its police power or its power of control over insane persons for the welfare of themselves and the general public, the state has no legal or constitutional right to hold in custody an insane person merely because he has been found to be insane. The Constitution still guarantees to him that his liberty shall not be taken away without due process of law, and if his own and the public welfare does not require it, he may not be deprived of his liberty by confinement in an institution. In the case of my husband, EZRA POUND, there is no reasonable possibility that he will recover his sanity, and, therefore, he can never be brought to trial under the indictment. It is also clear that his insanity is of a mild sort which does not require his continued hospitalization. Under these circumstances, if my husband is held indefinitely in confinement, he will in effect be confined for the rest of his life, solely because an indictment is pending against him which can never be resolved by trial.

15. It is a fundamental principle of law that every person is presumed to be innocent until he has been found guilty, and also that no person may be imprisoned until his guilt has been determined by process of law. Under these principles, the indictment against my husband is no evidence of his guilt, and he must be presumed innocent of the charge against him, and such presumption will endure for the rest of his life, because he will never be in condition for trial. As a result, a presumably innocent man is being held in confinement and will be confined for life, merely because he has been charged with crime, and has not sufficient mental capacity to meet the charge. His confinement on such grounds is nowhere authorized by statute, or by any principle

of law, and would deprive him of his liberty without due process of law in violation of the Fifth Amendment to the United States Constitution.

WHEREFORE, your petitioner prays that a Writ of Habeas Corpus be issued by this court directed to DR. WINFRED OVERHOLSER, Superintendent of St. Elizabeths Hospital, to produce the body of EZRA POUND before this court, at a time and place to be specified therein, then and there to receive and do what this court shall order concerning the detention and restraint of EZRA POUND, and that he shall be ordered to be discharged from the custody of the respondent and released to the care of the petitioner, as the Committee of his person and estate.

The writ was never issued. Mr. Cornell thought there was a good chance of a reversal on appeal, and so advised Mrs. Pound. She replied at once, asking him to suspend proceedings; her husband, she said, was not fit to appear in court—"the least thing shakes his nerves up terribly." She preferred to wait "until the November elections are over." The matter was not pursued again.

—————————— **2** ——————————

That year, by a gift from the Bollingen Foundation, the Library of Congress established the Bollingen Prize in Poetry to be awarded to the author of a book of verse which "in the opinion of the jury of selection, represents the highest achievement of American poetry in the year for which the award is made." With the prize went $1,000.

The jury, consisting of Léonie Adams, Conrad Aiken, W. H. Auden, Louise Bogan, Katherine Garrison Chapin (Mrs. Francis Biddle), T. S. Eliot, Paul Green, Robert Lowell, Katherine Anne Porter, Karl Shapiro, Theodore Spencer, Allen Tate, Willard Thorp and Robert Penn Warren—all of them Fellows in American Letters of the Library of Congress—awarded the first Bollingen Prize to Ezra Pound for *The Pisan Cantos*. A press release, February 20, 1949, stated:

"The Fellows are aware that objections may be made to awarding a prize to a man situated as is Mr. Pound. In their view, however, the possibility of such objection did not alter the responsibility assumed by the Jury of Selection. This was to make a choice for the award among the eligible books, provided any one merited such recognition, according to the stated terms of the Bollingen Prize. To permit other considerations than that of poetic achievement to sway the decision would destroy the significance of the award and would in principle deny the validity of that objective perception of value on which civilized society must rest."

Karl Shapiro voted against Pound in the balloting, "in the belief that the poet's political and moral philosophy ultimately vitiates his poetry and lowers its standards as literary work."

The critic Dwight Macdonald defended the award as "the brightest political act in a dark period."

All of the statements, it may be thought, are debatable.

1. Pound could have been honored, but a younger poet helped.

2. Mr. Shapiro does not know the political and moral philosophy of the authors of some of the greatest work in our literature, since we do not know who the authors were.

3. *The Pisan Cantos* were published, not suppressed—not even censored.

The objections foreseen by the Fellows were widespread, with the lamentable outcome that the first literary prize ever awarded by an agency of the United States government turned out to be the last.

Pound continued to write, translate, and publish. Distinguished callers came: T. S. Eliot, E. E. Cummings, William Carlos Williams, and a host of writers and poets from abroad, and of undergraduates at home. Two authors who were members of Congress became interested.

The first was Richard L. Neuberger of Oregon, the "unidentified Senator" who, on August 13, 1957, asked the Library of Congress for a study of the Pound case. The second was Representative Usher L. Burdick of North Dakota, who had been reared among the Sioux Indians, and was the author of many books about the Old West. On August 21, Representative Burdick introduced House Resolution 103, which was referred to the Committee on Rules. The resolution was explicit:

Whereas Ezra Pound has been incarcerated in Saint Elizabeths Hospital for the past twelve years on the assumption that he is insane; and

Whereas many people visit him there and are convinced that he is not insane: Therefore be it

Resolved, That the Committee on the Judiciary, acting as a whole or by subcommittee, is authorized and directed to conduct a full and complete investigation and study of the sanity of Ezra Pound, in order to determine whether there is justification for his continued incarceration in Saint Elizabeths Hospital.

The committee never sat. Mr. Burdick referred the matter to the Legislative Reference Service of the Library of Congress, where the task of gathering material on Pound was assigned to a brilliant research assistant in the Senior Specialists Division, H. A. Sieber, twenty-six years old.

Mr. Sieber delivered to Senator Neuberger and Representative Burdick a voluminous document which, when summarized, was published in instalments in the *Congressional Record* in the spring of 1958. Its title was "The Medical, Legal, Literary and Political Status of Ezra (Loomis) Pound," afterward known as the Sieber Report. Copies were reproduced by the Library of Congress for circulation among members of Congress and in the Department of Justice. One went to Pound.

"I have always regarded package words as a pest. Notably the idiotic term 'anti-Semitism,' " he wrote Mr. Burdick. "It is an impertinence to call me an amateur economist," he added, underlining the sentence in red. Of a passage dealing with his broadcasts he wrote that he did "what I considered my duty in warning the U. S. against Roosevelt's hysteria." Also underlined in red: "I seem to have been moved by emotion at some points of broadcasts, but component of error is to be expected in most human actions."

His strictures notwithstanding, he expressed the hope that the Sieber Report would have wide circulation. What he wrote Sieber is unprintable.

Pound was free when he typed these letters.

fourteen

Dismissal of Indictment

———————————— **1** ————————————

"All things are a flowing
Sage Heracleitus says. . . ."
—Pound's "Hugh Selwyn Mauberley"

The final phase of the case is contained in the documents which follow. It was not until 1958 when, as Mr. Cornell believes, "the government came around to the same way of thinking as I did, at least as a practical matter if not a legal theory," that efforts to free Pound were successful. The passage of time and the pressures exerted by many distinguished men of letters helped.

Thurman Arnold, of the renowned Washington law firm of Arnold, Fortas, and Porter, was now Pound's counsel. By a coincidence, Mr. Arnold had been a student at Wabash College in

Crawfordsville, Indiana, when Pound was teaching there; by another, he had also been Mr. Cornell's professor of law at Yale Law School. On April 14, 1958, he filed a motion to dismiss the 1945 indictment, together with an affidavit by Dr. Winfred Overholser, a memorandum of points and authorities, and a statement by Robert Frost. A new element in Mr. Arnold's motion and accompanying documents was the probability that Pound had been insane at the time he made the broadcasts; another was the difficulty the government would face in producing witnesses for any future prosecution of the case.

UNITED STATES DISTRICT COURT

FOR THE DISTRICT OF COLUMBIA

UNITED STATES OF AMERICA

v.

EZRA POUND, Defendant

Criminal No. 76028

Motion to Dismiss Indictment

Comes now Ezra Pound, defendant, through his committee, Mrs. Dorothy Shakespear Pound, and moves that the indictment in the above-entitled proceeding be dismissed.

And for grounds of the said motion, he respectfully represents:

1. On November 26, 1945, defendant was indicted on charges of treason relating to certain radio broadcasts made by defendant in Italy during World War II. On November 27, 1945, he stood mute on arraignment and a plea of not guilty to that indictment was entered by the Court. On December 4, 1945, defendant was admitted to Gallinger Hospital. On December 14, 1945, in pursuance of an appointment by this Court, Drs. Winfred Overholser, Marion R. King, Joseph L. Gilbert and Wendell Muncie submitted a joint written report to the Court that they had thoroughly examined the defendant on several occasions between December 4 and December 13, 1945, that it was their unani-

mous opinion that defendant was suffering from a paranoid state which rendered him mentally unfit to advise properly with counsel or to participate intelligently and reasonably in his own defense, and that he was insane and mentally unfit for trial. On January 18, 1946, the Court heard and granted a motion for a formal statutory inquisition to determine defendant's sanity. On February 13, 1946, the Court held such formal inquisition at which the jury, after hearing the evidence, report and conclusions of Drs. Overholser, King, Gilbert and Muncie, entered a formal verdict that the defendant was of unsound mind. Following that verdict, the defendant was committed to the custody of the United States and confined in Saint Elizabeths Hospital.

2. The defendant has remained in confinement at Saint Elizabeths Hospital since that time, where he has been the subject of constant and intense psychiatric tests, examinations, observation and study. As a result thereof, it is the opinion and conclusion of officials of Saint Elizabeths Hospital that defendant remains mentally unfit to advise properly with counsel or to participate intelligently and reasonably in his own defense and that he is insane and mentally unfit for trial, or to comprehend the nature of the charges against him.

3. Furthermore, it is the opinion and conclusion of these same officials that defendant's condition is permanent and incurable, that it cannot and will not respond to treatment and that trial on the charges against him will be forever impossible because of insanity.

4. Defendant is 72 years old. If the indictment against him is not dismissed he will die in Saint Elizabeths Hospital. He can never be brought to a state of mental competency or sanity sufficient to advise properly with counsel, to participate intelligently and reasonably in his own defense or to comprehend the nature of the charges against him. There can be no benefit to the United States in maintaining him indefinitely in custody as a public charge because that custody cannot contribute to his recovery and defendant's release would not prejudice the interests of the United States. The inevitable effect of failure to dismiss the indictment will be life imprisonment on account of alleged acts and events which can never be put to proof.

5. The primary alleged acts and events on which the indictment is based occurred prior to July 25, 1943. In the ensuing fifteen years memories have faded and direct evidence by the constitutionally-established minimum of two witnesses to each of the various alleged acts and events have inevitably dissipated. In all probability, therefore, the United States lacks sufficient evidence to warrant a prosecution at this time.

6. Suitable arrangements for defendant's custody and care are otherwise available. In the event that the indictment is dismissed, Mrs. Dorothy Shakespear Pound, committee, proposes to apply for the delivery of the defendant from further confinement at Saint Elizabeths Hospital to her restraint and care with bond under such terms and conditions as will be appropriate to the public good and the best interests and peace of mind of the defendant in the remaining years of his life.

7. On the issues of fact thus presented, defendant respectfully requests a hearing.

WHEREFORE, Ezra Pound, defendant, by his committee, Mrs. Dorothy Shakespear Pound, respectfully moves that the indictment be dismissed.

Affidavit

DR. WINFRED OVERHOLSER, being first duly sworn, deposes and says:

1. I am the Superintendent of Saint Elizabeths Hospital, Washington, District of Columbia.

2. Ezra Pound was admitted to Gallinger Hospital, Washington, District of Columbia, on December 4, 1945. Between that date and December 13, 1945, I and Drs. Joseph L. Gilbert, Marion R. King and Wendell Muncie each examined Ezra Pound on several occasions, separately and together, pursuant to appointment by the Honorable Bolitha J. Laws, Chief Justice, United States District Court. On December 14, 1945, I and Drs. Gilbert, King and Muncie submitted our joint report to the Chief Justice that Ezra Pound was suffering from a paranoid state which rendered him unfit to advise properly with counsel or to participate intelligently and reasonably in his own defense, and that he was insane and mentally unfit for trial on the criminal charges then pending against him. A copy of this joint report is attached hereto as Exhibit A.

3. On February 13, 1946, I testified to like effect at a formal inquisition as to sanity in respect to Ezra Pound.

4. Pursuant to the determination and verdict of the jury at the aforesaid inquisition, that Ezra Pound was of unsound mind, he was committed to Saint Elizabeths Hospital.

5. I have on a large number of occasions, both alone and with other psychiatrists of the staff of Saint Elizabeths Hospital and others, intensively tested, examined, observed and studied Ezra Pound.

6. If called to testify on a hearing in respect to dismissal of the pending criminal indictment against Ezra Pound, I will testify and state under oath that Ezra Pound is, and since December 4, 1945, has been, suffering from a paranoid state which has rendered and now renders

him unfit to advise properly with counsel or to participate intelligently and reasonably in his own defense, and that he was and is, and has continuously been, insane and mentally unfit for trial.

7. Furthermore, if called to testify on a hearing, I will testify and state under oath that the condition of Ezra Pound as thus described is permanent and incurable, that it will not and has not responded to treatment, that further professional therapeutic attention under hospital conditions would be of no avail and produce no beneficial results and that he is permanently and incurably insane.

8. Furthermore, if called to testify on a hearing, I will testify and state under oath that there is no likelihood, and indeed in my considered judgment and opinion no possibility, that the indictment pending against Ezra Pound can ever be tried because of the permanent and incurable condition of insanity of Ezra Pound, and that Ezra Pound will die insane in Saint Elizabeths Hospital without trial of the charges against him if the indictment remains pending.

9. Finally, if called to testify on a hearing, I will testify and state under oath that in my opinion, from examination of Ezra Pound made in 1945, within two to three years of the crimes charged in the indictment, there is a strong probability that the commission of the crimes charged was the result of insanity, and I would therefore seriously doubt that prosecution could show criminal responsibility even if it were hypothetically assumed that Ezra Pound could regain sufficient sanity to be tried.

10. In the event that the indictment is dismissed, I will recommend the delivery of Ezra Pound from further confinement at Saint Elizabeths Hospital under suitable arrangements for his custody, care and restraint by his committee, Mrs. Dorothy Shakespear Pound. Further confinement can serve no therapeutic purpose. It would be a needless expense and burden upon the public facilities of the hospital. Ezra Pound is not a dangerous person and his release would not endanger the safety of other persons or the officers, the property, or other interests of the United States.

Memorandum of Points and Authorities
in Support of Motion to Dismiss

1. The motion to dismiss the indictment is properly addressed to the Court. The Court has inherent power to dismiss an indictment in circumstances where justice requires and where, as here, the United States will never be able to prosecute. *United States* v. *Pack,* 20 F.R.D. 209

(D. Del. 1957); *United States* v. *Janitz,* 161 F.2d 19 (3d Cir. 1947). In a case such as this where the defendant is insane and in federal custody the Court has a special responsibility and authority over the proceedings, since such a defendant during commitment stands in the position of a ward of the Court. *United States* v. *Morris,* 154 F. Supp. 695 (S.D. Cal. 1957).

2. The motion presents an appeal to the discretion of the Court. For this reason, we ask leave to lodge the attached Statement of Robert Frost, who, along with many other poets and writers of distinction, has sought the release of Ezra Pound for the last several years. Although his statement does not speak to the legal issues raised, it is directly relevant to the serious considerations bearing upon this Court's exercise of its discretion.

Respectfully submitted,
THURMAN ARNOLD
WILLIAM D. ROGERS

Statement of Robert Frost

I am here to register my admiration for a government that can rouse in conscience to a case like this. Relief seems in sight for many of us besides the Ezra Pound in question and his faithful wife. He has countless admirers the world over who will rejoice in the news that he has hopes of freedom. I append a page or so of what they have been saying lately about him and his predicament. I myself speak as much in the general interest as in his. And I feel authorized to speak very specially for my friends, Archibald MacLeish, Ernest Hemingway and T. S. Eliot. None of us can bear the disgrace of our letting Ezra Pound come to his end where he is. It would leave too woeful a story in American literature. He went very wrongheaded in his egotism, but he insists it was from patriotism—love of America. He has never admitted that he went over to the enemy any more than the writers at home who have despaired of the Republic. I hate such nonsense and can only listen to it as an evidence of mental disorder. But mental disorder is what we are considering. I rest the case on Dr. Overholser's pronouncement that Ezra Pound is not too dangerous to go free in his wife's care, and too insane ever to be tried—a very nice distinction.

Mr. Thurman Arnold admirably put this problem of a sick man being held too long in prison to see if he won't get well enough to be tried for a prison offense. There is probably legal precedent to help toward a solution of the problem. But I should think it would have to be reached more by magnanimity than by logic and it is chiefly on magnanimity I am counting. I can see how the Department of Justice would hesitate in the matter from fear of looking more just to a great poet than it would be to a mere nobody. The bigger the Department the longer it might have to take thinking things through.

Appended to the statement were remarks by John Dos Passos, Van Wyck Brooks, Marianne Moore, Ernest Hemingway, Carl Sandburg, W. H. Auden, T. S. Eliot, Archibald MacLeish, Robert Fitzgerald, Allen Tate, Dag Hammarskjøld and Richard H. Rovere; some were from a brochure issued on Pound's seventieth birthday, the rest from correspondence in *Esquire,* following Mr. Rovere's article about Pound in the September, 1957, issue.

2

The motion was heard by Chief Judge Laws on April 18. Present in the courtroom were Pound, his wife, and son. Pound, who sat in the back, was dressed in an old blue jacket, tan sports shirt with the tails hanging out, and blue slacks.

Mr. Arnold told the Court that he represented not only Mrs. Pound, but "the world community of poets and writers." United States Attorney Oliver Gasch, now a judge in the District Court, said the motion was in the interest of justice "and should be granted."

When the order dismissing the indictment was handed down, Mrs. Pound left her place at counsels' table, walked to the rear of the courtroom, and kissed her husband.

Order Dismissing Indictment

This cause came on for hearing on defendant's motion to dismiss the indictment and upon consideration of the affidavit of Dr. Winfred Overholser, the Superintendent of St. Elizabeths Hospital, and it appearing to the Court that the defendant is presently incompetent to stand trial and that there is no likelihood that this condition will in the foreseeable future improve, and it further appearing to the Court that there is available to the defense psychiatric testimony to the effect that there is a strong probability that the commission of the crimes charged was the result of insanity, and it appearing that the Government is not in a position to challenge this medical testimony, and it further appearing that the Government consents to the dismissal of this indictment, it is by the Court this 18th day of April, 1958,

ORDERED that the indictment be and the same is hereby dismissed.

Bolitha J. Laws
CHIEF JUDGE

Presented by
Thurman Arnold
William D. Rogers
COUNSEL FOR THE DEFENDANT
I consent
Oliver Gasch
UNITED STATES ATTORNEY

The same day the American Civil Liberties Union forwarded identical letters to the Attorney General and the Secretary of the Department of Health, Education and Welfare which, in effect, summed up the important issues of the Pound case—alleged treason aside—as they may affect or concern the ordinary citizen.

AMERICAN CIVIL LIBERTIES UNION
170 Fifth Avenue
New York, 10, N.Y.

April 18, 1958

Mr. William P. Rogers, Attorney General
Department of Justice
Washington, D.C.

and

Mr. Marion B. Folsom, Secretary
Department of Health, Education and Welfare
Washington, D.C.

Re: *Ezra Pound*

Dear Sirs:
We have just received word that Ezra Pound has been released from

commitment under criminal court order to St. Elizabeths Hospital pending his ability to stand trial under a criminal indictment for treason. We understand from statements in the press that the government did not oppose the motion for such release.

We highly commend your decision not to interpose such opposition. We, like many others, have been deeply disturbed by the anomalous situation in a democracy whereby a person could, in effect, be incarcerated for life by a criminal court without any conviction for crime. That this situation was exemplified in the Ezra Pound case in a fortuitous demonstration of a common practice both in the federal courts and in virtually all state jurisdictions. We recognize that you have taken cognizance of this specific problem in the specific case of Ezra Pound and certainly approve of your decision not to oppose the motion to quash his indictment.

We hope that you will now review your overall policy in this field. Many persons of lesser or no prominence are similarly affected. As far as the Department of Justice is concerned, we suggest that it periodically review all pending cases that have been temporarily disposed of by commitment pending mental ability to stand trial with the view of suggesting to the court, on its own motion, that the case be quashed. As far as the Department of Health, Education and Welfare is concerned, we suggest that in view of the fact that the Secretary is charged with the legal responsibility of reporting to the court when a person under indictment in its custody is capable of standing trial that it should assume the concomitant responsibility to report to the court when, in its judgment, such person is determined to be permanently mentally incompetent and, therefore, permanently incapable of standing trial.

We believe that such actions by you will contribute materially to a regularizing of the procedure established in the Ezra Pound case. We believe that they will be a material contribution to the protection of the civil rights of the mentally incompetent.

Sincerely yours,
PATRICK MURPHY MALIN
Executive Director

At the home of Representative Usher L. Burdick, surrounded by photographers and reporters, Pound talked for seventy-five minutes, after which he remarked to the congressman: "I don't have to tell it all in one day. I can come back. But you've had a chance to talk as much as you like. It is what you're paid for. I've had the plug in for twelve years."

He was wearing an open-necked cotton shirt with short sleeves, green cotton trousers, and brown shoes only partly laced. A small canvas bag hung by a string around his neck; in it were two pairs of glasses.

He talked about his grandfather, the congressman from Wisconsin, and called for "some of the sanity of the Greenback Party," meaning fiat money. About two Presidents: "I thought when Herbert Hoover came into the White House the prejudices against expatriates might diminish a little." Mr. Hoover had lived in Kensington, but did not meet Pound. "You know, Ike invited me to dinner once. Yes, when he was president of Columbia. I was a member of the Academy of Social and Political Sciences. He didn't know what he was signing. I was in the hellhole at the time."

About Jews: "I am not anti-Semitic. I have been making jokes about Jews all my life. Fifty years ago we had jokes about the Scotch and the Irish and the Jews, and the best stories you got were from the Jews." He suddenly remembered one of them from his Kensington days. "I would trust Mr. Cournos a damned sight more than Winston Churchill."

What he said on the air: "I never told the troops not to fight. What I am interested in is the American Constitution."

A reporter asked him how he felt about Frost's help in freeing him.

"He ain't been in much of a hurry," Pound replied.

It is now well known that the moving force behind the freeing of Pound was the man he attacked in his April 23, 1942 broadcast, Archibald MacLeish, who declines all comment.

Postscript

Aged seventy-three, Pound returned with his wife to Italy on the *Cristoforo Colombo*. He stayed first at the home of his daughter in Merano, where he continued to work on the *Cantos,* passing the goal of one hundred he had set himself in Kensington half a century before. Then he divided his time between Rapallo, in the summer, and Venice, in the winter, settling finally in Sant' Ambrogio, in the hills to which the Germans had driven him and where the *partigiani* had come to arrest him.

Other places knew him—Darmstadt, where a performance of his *Women of Trachis,* completed in St. Elizabeths, was given; Rome; Trento, which made him an honorary citizen; Spoleto, where his opera on Villon was produced at Gian Carlo Menotti's Festival of Two Worlds; Paris, where, stooped and ailing, he was reported to have expressed remorse; London, where he attended memorial services for T. S. Eliot in Westminster Abbey. From London he went to Dublin to see the widow of William Butler Yeats. He had been best man at their wedding.

He wrote to Richard Aldington:

Cher R/
    amid cumulative fatigue, and much that is gone to muddle. thinking of early friendship and late. This is to say I have for you a lasting affection.

E. P.

One day, while he was wintering in Venice, a reporter asked Pound: "Where are you living now?"

"In hell," he replied.

"Which hell?"

"Here, here," he exclaimed, placing both hands over his heart.

index

Abramson, Benjamin, 105
Adams, Henry Brooks, 65
Adams, John, 32, 44, 89
Adams, Léonie, 187
Aiken, Conrad, 89, 90, 187
Aldington, Richard, 20, 21, 24, 27, 45, 200
Alexander, Field Marshal Earl, 69, 70
Allen, Robert L., 73
American Academy of Social and Political Science, 65, 199
American Civil Liberties Union, 197
Anderson, Donald, 105, 107
Antheil, George, 23
Aponte, Salvatore, 81
Aristotle, 11

Arnold, Thurman, 17, 190, 191, 195, 197
Arthur, Chester A., 14
Auden, W. H., 187, 196

Balfour, Arthur, 30
Baruch, Bernard M., 50
Bankhead, W. B., 37
Beerbohm, Sir Max, 28
Behrman, S. N., 28
Benét, William Rose, 90
Bennett, James V., 133, 134
Berry, William T., 105
Biddle, Francis, 63, 67, 187
Binyon, Laurence, 18
Bogan, Louise, 187

205

Bollingen Prize in Poetry, 187, 188
Borah, William E., 37
Bottome, Phyllis, 21
Bridges, H. Styles, 38
British Broadcasting Corp., 12, 53, 63
Broadus, Thomas H., 105
Brooks, Van Wyck, 196
Bruni, Giuseppe, 80, 81
Bunting, Basil, 34
Burdick, Usher L., 188, 189, 198
Burr, Aaron, 88
Byrd, Harry F., 38

Calhoun, John Caldwell, 58
Cavalcanti, Guido, 29
Cerf, Bennett, 91
Chapin, Katherine Garrison, 187
"Charter Oak," 14
Chaucer, Geoffrey, 31
Christie, Ethel M., 105
Churchill, Winston S., 6, 12, 45, 55, 69, 73, 199
Commager, Henry Steele, 45
Commins, Saxe, 90
Confucius, 6, 10, 11, 64, 96, 113, 119, 149
Congress, Library of, 61, 187, 189
Cornell, Julien, 92, 93, 103, 105, 107, 182, 184, 187, 190, 191
Coughlin, Charles E., 41
Cournos, John, 22, 24, 27, 39, 199
Cowley, Malcolm, 23
Cowley, W. H., 43, 44
Cummings, E. E., 37, 39, 41, 83, 188

Davies, Joseph E., 76
Devers, Gen. Jacob L., 66, 67
de Born, Bertran, 19
de Leonardis, Fernando, 80, 81
de Vega, Lope, 16
Dickinson, Emily, 88
Disciplinary Training Center, 70, 71, 73, 76, 93, 95, 104

District of Columbia Jail, 76, 93, 103
Donovan, Gen. William J., 50
Dos Passos, John, 196
Douglas, Maj. C. H., 24, 29, 31, 33, 45
Downey, Sheridan, 38

Eastman, Max, 41
Eisenhower, Dwight D., 199
Eliot, T. S., 21, 22, 23, 43, 88, 187, 188, 195, 196, 200
Ente Italiano Audizione Radiofoniche, 4, 9

Farley, James A., 7
Federal Bureau of Investigation, 67, 68, 69, 74
Federal Communications Commission, 8, 47
Fenollosa, Ernest, 12
Fish, Hamilton, 58
Fitzgerald, Robert, 196
Folsom, Marion B., 197
Ford, Ford Madox, 19, 22, 28, 40
Foreign Broadcast Intelligence Service, 8
Frost, Robert, 20, 191, 195, 199

Gallinger Hospital, 103, 110, 116, 125, 127, 128, 131, 132, 147, 148, 149, 164, 165, 166, 167, 172, 179, 184, 191, 193
Gasch, Oliver, 196, 197
Gaudier-Brzeska, Henri, 23, 26, 29
Gesell, Silvio, 32, 33, 39, 46
Gilbert, Dr. Joseph L., 104, 105, 128, 131, 148, 163, 178, 184, 191, 192, 193
Giovagnoli, Armando, 80
Glass, Carter, 58
Goldring, Douglas, 22
Gonne, Maude, 28
Green, Paul, 187

Gregory, Lady, 21, 27
Gruesen, John J., 71, 72

H. D. (Hilda Doolittle), 20
Hamilton College, 16, 42, 43
Hammarskjöld, Dag, 196
Hargrave, John, 40
Hemingway, Ernest, 23, 37, 195, 196
Hewlett, Maurice, 18
Heyman, Katherine Ruth, 18
Himmler, Heinrich, 6
Hitler, Adolph, 6, 13, 30, 36, 51, 69, 84, 182
Hoover, Herbert, 199
Hull, Cordell, 56, 57
Hunt, Violet, 22, 26
Hyde-Lees, Georgie (Mrs. W. B. Yeats), 27

James, Alice, 53
James, Henry, 53, 86
James, William, 86
Jefferson, Thomas, 31, 32, 33, 89
Jenkins, Carroll K., 105
Johnson, Andrew, 44
Johnson, Samuel, 4, 92
Jowitt, Earl, 3
Joyce, James, 23, 37
Justice, Department of, 47, 48, 103

Kaltenborn, H. V., 43, 44
Keats, John, 27
Keynes, John Maynard, 12
King, Dr. Marion R., 104, 105, 127, 129, 148, 164, 172, 178, 184, 191, 192, 193
Kitson, Arthur, 65
Knox, Frank, 50
Krylenko, Eliena (Mrs. Max Eastman), 41
Kuhn, Loeb & Co., 59

Laughlin, James, 40, 92

Lawrence, D. H., 19
Lawrenson, Raymond M., 105
Laws, Hon. Bolitha J., 76, 93, 103, 104, 105, 107, 182, 193, 196
Lehman, Herbert H., 49
Lewis, Wyndham, 27
Lincoln, Abraham, 31, 33
Litvinov, Maxim, 54
Lodge, Henry Cabot, 38
Longfellow, Henry Wadsworth, 14
"Loomis Gang," 15, 16
Lowe, E. A., 28
Lowell, Robert, 187
Luzzi, Fernando, 81

Macdonald, Dwight, 188
MacLeish, Archibald, 38, 48, 49, 50, 51, 195, 196, 199
MacMillan Commission, 65
Malin, Patrick Murphy, 198
Marceron, Frank A., 105
Martowicz, Edward T., 105
Marx, Karl, 44
Mathews, Elkin, 20
Matlack, Isaiah, 93, 103, 105, 107
Matthiessen, F. O., 88
Mencken, H. L., 41
Menotti, Gian Carlo, 200
Miller, Charles A., 42
Missear, Jesse W., 105
Mohler, Edward A., 105
Monroe, Harriet, 20, 21, 27, 88
Montgomery, Gen. Bernard L., 54
Morgenthau, Henry, Jr., 49, 50
Moore, Marianne, 196
Moore, Mary, 17, 18
Morris, Leonard W., 105
Muncie, Dr. Wendell, 103, 104, 105, 106, 131, 134, 150, 179, 183, 184, 193
Munson, Gorham B., 39, 40
Mussolini, Benito, 4, 9, 26, 29, 30, 31, 32, 37, 39, 44, 51, 68, 69, 73, 154

Neuberger, Richard L., 188, 189
Nevins, Allan, 45

Orage, Alfred Richard, 24
Overholser, Dr. Winfred, 104, 105, 127, 131, 146, 162, 164, 178, 183, 191, 192, 193, 196

Packard, Eleanor, 8, 9
Packard, Reynolds, 8, 9, 10
PM, x, 94, 103
Pennsylvania, University of, 16, 17
Picabia, Francis, 37
Picasso, Pablo, 37
Poetry: A Magazine of Verse, 20, 47, 88
Polen, George E., 105
Polytechnic Institute, 18
Porter, Katherine Anne, 187
Pound, Angevine Loomis, 15
Pound, Dorothy (Mrs. Ezra Pound), x, 22, 27, 91, 97, 181, 182, 183, 191, 193, 196
Pound, Mary (Mrs. Boris de Rachewiltz), 35, 97, 200
Pound, Homer Loomis, 11, 14, 15, 16, 28, 34
Pound, Isabel Weston (Mrs. Homer Loomis Pound), 14, 15, 16, 28
Pound, Omar Shakespear, 27, 35, 196
Pound, Thaddeus Coleman, 15, 30

Rhys, Ernest, 18
Rogers, J. H., 29
Rogers, William D., 195, 197
Rogers, William P., 197
Rommel, Field Marshal Erwin, 54
Roosevelt, Franklin Delano, 6, 7, 9, 13, 29, 32, 37, 42, 43, 48, 50, 51, 55, 57, 58, 68
Root, Edward, 42
Rothenstein, Sir William, 21
Rovere, Richard H., 196

St. Elizabeths Hospital, 104, 105, 125, 131, 132, 147, 148, 149, 165, 166, 178, 181, 182, 183, 184, 187, 192, 193, 194
Sandburg, Carl, 88, 196
Sanders, Al, 56
Santayana, George, 71, 72
Serly, Tibor, 41, 42
Shakespear, Henry Hope, 22
Shakespear, Olivia, 22, 27, 35
Shakespeare, William, 31
Shapiro, Karl, 187, 188
Shaw, George Bernard, 18
Sieber, H. A., 189
Sinclair, May, 18
Sitwell, Sir Osbert, 21, 28
Slocum, John, 39, 44
Smith, Lawrence M. C., 66
Spencer, Theodore, 40, 187
Stalin, Josef, 51, 173
State, Department of, x, 5
Stein, Gertrude, 23
Stimson, Henry L., 50

Tagore, Rabindranath, 21
Tate, Allen, 187, 196
Thorp, Willard, 187
Tinkham, George Holden, 38, 42
Toklas, Alice B., 23
Trotsky, Leon, 44

Ulio, Maj. Gen. J. A., 66, 67
Ungaro, Adriano, 81
United Nations, 60, 92

Van Buren, Martin, 32, 89
Vatican Library, 28
Voorhis, H. J., 38

Wabash College, 16, 17
Wadsworth, Joseph, 14
Wallace, Henry A., 12, 13, 38
Walpole, Hugh, 22

Warren, Robert Penn, 187
Washington, George, 33
Welles, Sumner, 55, 56, 57
Wellesley, Lady Dorothy, 35
Wells, H. G., 6, 45, 46
Williams, William Carlos, 16, 18, 19, 84, 188

Wilson, Woodrow, 7, 45

Yeats, William Butler, 11, 21, 27, 30, 35, 88, 200

Zanchetti, Walter, 80
Zukofsky, Louis, 34, 35, 39, 41, 87

The Case of
EZRA POUND

by Charles Norman

That great "maker" Ezra Pound—perhaps the most influential shaper of the modern sensibility in the poetry of the English-speaking world—is also a *case,* personal and legal. The paradoxical character of the man, combining the rarest generosity and parochial spleen, commanding intellect and backwoods bigotry, esthetic seemliness and political monstrosity, appears as if designed to illustrate the mystery of the human personality.

Charles Norman, poet, man of letters, and distinguished biographer of such figures as E. E. Cummings, has already presented a full-length portrait of the man and his work in his *Ezra Pound.* Significant new information about the attempts to have the poet tried for treason justifies his taking up the subject once more. He focuses on the cause *célèbre* of Pound's incarceration in a *mental* hospital while the question of his sanity and fitness to stand trial was debated by lawyers and psychiatrists. Documents and testimony, previously unavailable, conclusively demonstrate the fallaciousness of a widespread assumption about the